Teaching the English Language to Primary Students

Tasks for classroom interaction

초등영어교수법

교실 상호작용을 위한 과업

Teaching the English Language to Primary Students

Tasks for Classroom Interaction

김영태 지음

초등영어교수법 교실 상호작용을 위한 과업

Global Contents

Preface

Teaching the English language to primary students : tasks for classroom interaction is mainly written for students of universities of education. This book can be used as a textbook for 'practices of teaching English to primary students.' It can also be used for graduate students majoring in English language teaching and learning. Finally, the information in this book can be applied to people in charge of teaching English to children in private institutes as well as commercial materials developers.

Teaching the English language to primary students focuses on teaching language skills in primary English classrooms. Therefore, the priority is the practices of teaching and learning in the classroom, not the theoretical background of each language skill. Hopefully this book helps primary English teachers to teach students in English in their classrooms.

This book consists of three parts. The first part includes teaching the four language skills - listening, speaking, reading and writing. Each chapter is based on an analysis of the former primary English textbooks. And the second part emphasizes teaching activities using the four language skills - songs, play, stories and role play. The teaching ideas of each chapter hopefully encourages the readers to apply these ideas to their classrooms. Finally, the last part is designed for preparing lesson plans for primary English classrooms. It includes ways to write lesson plans for class and examples of lesson plans written by primary teachers themselves.

This book would not have been possible without the insight and support of undergraduate students, graduate students, colleagues and friends. First, I'm indebted to Sujin Kim, my former graduate student and primary teacher, for enabling me to include practices of interactions between the teacher and students in the primary English classroom. I also would like to thank Ingrid Zwaal for her comments on the first drafts of this book and for providing critical insights for teaching English to children. A special thanks goes to Dr. Doobon Pae for his personal and academic support. Even though they gave me insights and help for this book, I am solely responsible for the final version of this book (including any errors). Most of all, I'm deeply indebted to Jeongpyo Hong, president of Global Contents Publishing Company and the editors for their careful work.

Finally, my deepest gratitude goes to my best friend and wife, Mija Hwang and my son, Hoyong, for their support and encouragement.

Contents

Part I Teaching the four language skills

Part II Teaching activities using the four language skills

Part III Planning lessons

Part I

Teaching the four language skills

1. Teaching Listening

2. Teaching Speaking

3. Teaching Reading

4. Teaching Writing

1 Teaching Listening

In this chapter, we will try to solve the following questions concerning teaching listening in primary classrooms:

1) What is listening?
2) When do we listen to others in everyday life?
3) Through what route do we reach listening comprehension?
4) What are good tips for primary English teachers to teach listening in the classroom?
5) What are the main steps for teaching listening in the classroom?
6) What are the tasks for listening that can be used in the primary classroom?
7) Is there any model procedure for teaching listening in the classroom?

1. The definition of listening

What is listening? Let's suppose a person says the following sentence, and we don't know the appropriate context.

Ex) A: It's very hot in here.

What does this example mean? It may mean one of the following according to the context where it is produced:

- the fact that it is very hot
- asking someone to open the window, to turn the fan on or to bring something cold to drink, etc.
- complaining because the person has never predicted this hot weather

Then, in order to listen successfully to the spoken language, how does the listener figure out what he/she has heard? First, listeners need to be able to perceive sounds, words and sentences by the ear. We call this process 'hearing.'

The listener also must recognize and interpret what he/she has heard using the context and background knowledge. Therefore, listening is not a passive process but an active and interpretive process. Hearing is simply paying attention to what is heard. In contrast, listening is the activity of paying attention to and trying to interpret what we hear. As Anderson & Lynch (1988, pp. 9~15) say, hearing is 'the listener as a tape recorder,' and listening 'the listener as an active model builder.' To successfully listen to the message, we should listen to the spoken language well besides just hearing it.

2. Real life listening situations

According to Hedge (2000, p. 228), in real life language use, approximately 9 percent is devoted to writing, 16 percent to reading, 30 percent to speaking, and 45 percent to listening. And many learners of English will find themselves in a variety of situations where they will listen to English being used in real life for different purposes (Anderson & Lynch, 1988; Underwood, 1989).

(1) Following a lesson (for example, in a school where English is one of the languages of instruction)
(2) Listening to the radio for entertainment
(3) Listening to CDs (of music, etc)
(4) Watching television for entertainment

(5) Listening to the telephone (to take a message, or simply to hold a conversation)
(6) Listening to live conversations in which one takes no part (usually referred to as 'eavesdropping')
(7) Listening to announcements (at airports, railway stations, etc), and the news, the weather forecast, etc. on the radio
(8) Watching a film in a cinema
(9) Following instructions (for example, in an assembly line)
(10) Listening to someone giving a public address (like a president's annual address)

Real life listening can be divided into two simple categories, one way listening where listeners do not have to speak and two way listening where listeners face the speakers. Therefore, we should prepare our students for those listening situations.

3. Models of listening comprehension

How can listeners reach listening comprehension? According to the L2 researchers (Anderson & Lynch, 1988; Brown, 2001; Flowerdew & Miller, 2005; Harmer, 2001; Hedge, 2000), they understand the message through either bottom-up processing, or top-down processing, or interactive processing.

1) The bottom-up model

- According to bottom-up processing, in order for listeners to understand the message, they should start by tackling the sounds, words, and structures. Without linguistic knowledge, he/she can not figure out what is heard.

2) The top-down model

- It emphasizes the use of contextual knowledge and background knowledge in processing a message rather than depending upon linguistic knowledge. Even though students do not have sufficient linguistic knowledge for understanding the text, he/she can predict what is heard.

3) The interactive model

- Today, L2 researchers and theorists agree that listening comprehension is processed simultaneously at different levels. Linguistic knowledge, contextual knowledge and schematic knowledge are involved interactively in this tough processing. But no one clearly explains how.

We can summarize the process of listening comprehension in the following Figure. 1.

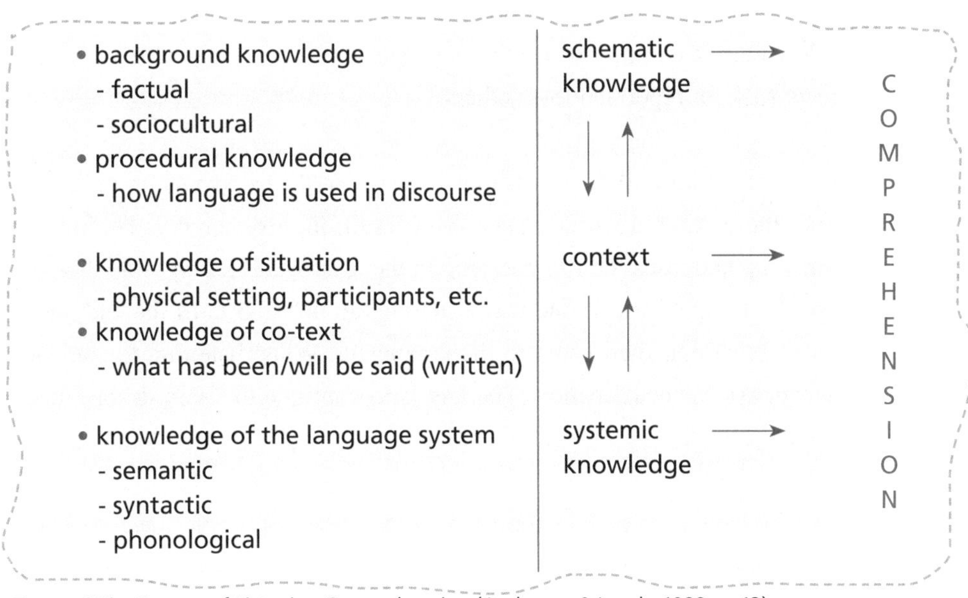

Figure. 1 The Process of Listening Comprehension (Anderson & Lynch, 1988, p. 13)

4. Guidelines for teaching listening to children

Teaching listening is distinctly different from teaching speaking. For example, a listener does not have the advantage that the speaker has with the strategies available from face to face interaction. Teachers and students must keep in mind the disadvantages of learning listening when trying to understand what is heard. What are the potential problems and how can we handle them to attain good listening comprehension? Here are some tips for listening comprehension based on Brown (2001) and Underwood (1989).

1) The listener cannot comprehend the words as fast as the speaker utters them, so what is heard depends more on the speaker than the listener. But do not forget that not every word is important. Listeners should focus on interpreting the message rather than understanding or interpreting each word.

2) Unlike face to face interaction, when watching TV or listening to the radio, the listener cannot get the speaker to repeat their words. However, in a classroom students learn quickly to ask the teacher for repetition. Therefore, students need to know how to ask for repetition from others.

3) Listeners may not know all the words in a message. So the listener stops and thinks about what the unknown word means. As a result, the listener falls behind and cannot catch up and loses the full meaning in the message. Keep in mind listeners who stop to think get lost. In one way listening, do not stop until the end and if you missed something then listen to the tape again. When listening to someone else, you can ask for clarification. The key is to continue to listen despite some ambiguity.

4) Listeners may have difficulty in coping with the 'signals' for conversation. There are many ways that a speaker can use to show that she/he is moving from one topic to another, showing an example or repeating a point, etc. For example, lecturers

usually clearly show that they are about to begin a new point. They employ expressions like 'Secondly...' or 'Then,...' They may move slightly, make a gesture or pause. They may mark a change to a new point by increased loudness, a clear change in pitch or a different intonation. Therefore, students need to learn to listen and watch, if the speaker is visible, for the 'signals' to be able to connect the various statements in the way the speaker meant them to be connected.

5) It is very difficult for students to understand the message clearly, especially when the students are not familiar with the target culture. Teachers can help students fill in the gaps of information by 'show and tell the differences' between the cultures. And teachers can compensate for any lack of knowledge by using nonverbal means such as facial expressions, gestures, eye contact, etc.

5. How to teach listening comprehension in the classroom

How can we teachers teach listening in the classroom? L2 researchers and practitioners suggest that teachers should follow the order of the pre-listening activities through the while-listening activities to the post-listening activities (Flowerdew & Miller, 2005; Hedge, 2000; Underwood, 1989). We will see the purposes and the specific tasks of each activity in the following.

1) The pre-listening activities

(1) Purpose: The teacher can help students get prepared for listening to the text and doing the tasks as well.

(2) Ideas for pre-listening activities

(a) Looking at the pictures and guessing what will be heard before listening

- Where are they? / Who are they? / What are they doing?

(b) Looking at the picture and finding out what the things are

- What's this/that? / What are these/those?

(c) Predicting words or expressions

- He looks very hungry. What does he say?

(d) Informal small class talk

- Give a small talk related to the picture

2) The while-listening activities

(1) Purpose: The teacher can help students to understand the spoken text and complete the tasks as well.

(2) Ideas for while-listening activities

(a) Marking the things in pictures

- Find the types of fruit and put ticks in the appropriate boxes.

(b) Finding the right picture

- Find the right picture that fits the description.

(c) Putting the pictures in order

- Listen carefully and put the pictures in order as to what is heard.

(d) Completing pictures

- Look at this unfinished picture of a room. Please add some more drawings according to the description and complete the picture.

(e) Carrying out actions

- Simon Says (Do as I say)

(f) Completing grids

- Find out how your friends come to school and put ticks in the appropriate boxes.

3) The post-listening activities

(1) Purpose: The teacher can help students to reflect on the listening activity. So, the teacher can give students more listening activities if they are needed. Or they can be engaged in additional listening tasks integrated with the other skills of speaking, reading and writing.

(2) Ideas for post-listening activities

(a) Listening to the text again

- You need more listening practice. How about listening to it again?

(b) Summarizing

- Tell us what is said about the boy.

(c) Reaction to what is heard

- How do you feel about the man?
- Do you agree with her? If yes, why?

(d) Role play

- Do a role play based on what you have heard.

6. Listening tasks

Primary English teachers invent a lot of listening tasks for helping children to understand what is said to them. The examples are 'Listen and Do,' 'Listen for the information,' 'Listen and Repeat,' and 'Listen and Say.'

1) Listen and do

(1) Instructions for class management

- Sit down please. / Look at the books. / Come to the board please.
- Give rulers out to the students.
- Walk to the board and write your name on it.

(2) Listen and point:

T : Point to the window.
Point to the door.
Point to the ceiling.
Point to Sumi.
Point to your teacher.

(3) Listen and move your body

T : Clap your hands.
Snap your fingers.
Slap your legs.
Stamp your feet.
Stand on your right foot.
Hop on your left foot five times.

(4) Listen and mime

Ex. 1) Mime everyday routines.

T: You're getting up … getting up. Good. You're stretching your arms … stretching your arms … Very good! Now, you're rubbing your eyes … rubbing your eyes. Very good! You're yawning … yawning. Finally, you go into the bathroom. You're brushing your teeth.

Ex. 2) Do as the leaders do!

T: OK, now get in a line. Sujin … you're here. Now Changho. Now Minji. Ok, now follow me. Come on … round the class. OK, we're walking, walking, walking. Now, jumping like a kangaroo, jumping, jumping. Yes, now flying. … like a plane. We're flying, flying, flying … down again. We're swimming … swimming in the sea … swimming. We're swimming in the sea.

Ex. 3) Let's pretend we're animals

T: OK, let's pretend we're animals. Everybody, stand up. Ready, here we go.
You're a bird, you fly high like a plane.
You're a cheetah, you run fast like a car.
You're a kangaroo, you jump high like a bouncy ball.

(5) Other activities

Ex. 1)

T: Listen carefully.
OK. Anyone who has grandfather, grandpa, raise your hand.

S: (Students with grandfathers raise their hands.)

T: Very good. Now, anyone who has uncles, stand up.

Ex. 2)

T: OK. Listen carefully and do as I say.
Here we go!
If you're happy, then clap your hands.

S: (Some students who look happy clap their hands.)

T: Well done! You look very happy.
This time, if you're hungry, touch your tummy, tummy.

S: (Some children touch their tummies.)

T: Well done! But, you two don't look hungry.

2) Listen for the information (based on Scott & Ytreberg, 1990, pp. 24~25)

(1) Listen and find the right picture

- Listen and find the right picture (and put a mark in the correct box.)

Ex. 1)

T: Do you know who she is? She has a striped brown shirt. Her shirt isn't spotted. It's striped. I like her striped brown shirt. Don't you think so? She has a striped brown shirt.

Ex. 2)

T: Listen carefully. Sunam, thanks. Are you ready? Here we go. Point to the picture I am talking about. I wonder if he's young or old. The young man has a cat in his arms. Not a dog. He has a cat in his arms.

S: (The children point)

T: Right! The young man has a cat.

(2) Listen and put the pictures in order.

- Give out a set of pictures which describe a story. The pictures are not arranged. Students are told to arrange the pictures in the order that is heard.

(3) Listen and put

- Students are given a diagram of a house with a kitchen, living room, bedroom and bathroom. They are given pictures of a bathtub, stove, sofa and a bed. They listen and place the furnishings according to directions.

T: The bathtub goes in the bathroom.
The stove goes in the kitchen.
The sofa belongs in the living room.
The bed should be in the bedroom.

- Instead of ready-made pictures, the students can draw the furnishings in the appropriate rooms.

(4) Listen and draw

Ex. 1) (based on Slattery & Willis, 2001, p. 33)

T: Now look at this picture. OK. It's a clown. Point to the nose. Where's his nose? Yes, there it is. His nose. Now, color the nose yellow.

Ss: *(Children color the nose yellow.)*

T: OK, everyone. Color the nose yellow. Very good. That's really nice. Good.

T: Now show me the eyes, the clown's eyes. Yes here they are. Now color the eyes brown. Great!

T: Now when you've finished, put up your hands. Are you finished? Very good.

T: OK, let's check now. Point to … Show me … Yellow nose, brown eyes … Very good. Now we'll put up the pictures on the wall. Very good, they're lovely. Now let's count. OK, let's see how many yellow noses we have. One, two, three, four …

Ex. 2)

T: Take out a piece of paper. We're going to draw pictures. Listen carefully and draw what you hear. Ready? Here we go!

- Draw a square in the middle.
- Then, on top of the square, draw a triangle. It's the roof of the house.
- Now, draw two windows, one on the left, and the other one on the right. And in the middle draw a door.
- Finally draw a tall tree on the left of the house.

(5) Listen for the mistakes

- The teacher describes the picture in your book but makes mistakes, so that students have to listen for the mistakes. When students spot the teacher's mistake, they correct the error and the teacher tells the corrected part again.

Ex. 1) Right or wrong?

T: OK, listen carefully.
Am I right or am I wrong?
If I'm right, clap once. If I'm wrong, shake your heads.
Ready? Go!
It's raining.
S: (Students clap.)
T: Right, it's raining. Today is Wednesday.
S: (Students shake their heads.)
T: Sorry, it's Thursday.
S: (Students shake their heads again.)
T: Silly me! It's Tuesday.

S: (Students clap.)

T: Right. Today is Tuesday. We'll have P.E. in the afternoon.

S: (Students shake their heads again.)

T: …

(6) Surveys

- Give out a table about students' last summer to students.
- The teacher says what each student did last summer.
- Each student finds the things that his/her friends did last summer, and put ticks in the appropriate boxes.

3) Listen and repeat

In order for students to get used to English pronunciation, teachers can ask them to listen and repeat rhymes and children's songs. The bottom line is how repetitive and interesting the rhymes and songs are.

(1) Rhymes (based on Scott & Ytreberg, 1990, p. 27)

Ex. 1)

Rain on the green grass,
Rain on the trees,
Rain on the house-tops,
But don't rain on me.

Ex. 2)

Rain, rain go away,
Come again another day.
Little Johnny wants to play.

Ex. 3)

I love coffee.
I love tea.
I hate the dentist.
and the dentist hates me.

(2) Songs (http://www.kiddiddles.com/lyrics)

Five little ducks went out one day
Over the hills and far away
Mother Duck said, "Quack, quack, quack, quack."
But only four little ducks came back.

4) Listen and say (based on Kim J-H et al, 2009)

(1) Look and choose

- The teacher describes a group of animals. Each student chooses one animal and tells what he chose.

Ex)

T: Choose an animal with four legs and a tail.
S1: A monkey.
S2: A tiger has four legs and a tail.
S3: This is a lion. It has four legs and a tail.
S4: I chose a bear. It has four legs and a tail.

(2) Listen and sort

- The teacher puts the animal picture cards on the board. They are elephant, crocodile, hippo, whale, zebra, tiger, shark, monkey.
- Tell the students to sort the animals as 'Land animals' and 'Water animals.'
- Then the students pick out elephant, zebra, monkey, and tiger, and they say 'Land animals!'

(3) Tennis game

- Make two teams of three students.
- A student from the first team (A1) says the name of an animal and a student from the other team (B1) responds with the name of another animal.
- The game goes on as long as the students can say animal names without repetition.

A1: Tiger.
B1: Monkey.
A2: Lion.
B2: Cow.

(4) Find the odd one out

- Listen carefully and then find out what does not belong with the others. Are you ready?

T: Apples, bananas, balls, fish
S: Balls.
T: You're right. We can eat apples, bananas, and fish, but we can't eat balls. We can play with balls.

(5) Guess my animal - actions/mime

- A student chooses an animal card and imitates the animal. For example, walk like the animal or make sounds like the animal.
- The student who first guesses the right answer comes to the front and continues the game.

7. Practice of teaching listening in the primary classroom

How do primary English teachers teach listening in their classrooms? We will see an example in the following. Ms. Kim teaches 'Look and Listen' of 'Lesson 4. Wash Your Hands (MEST, 2009, p. 38 (Elementary school English 3))' to third graders.

Dialog 1

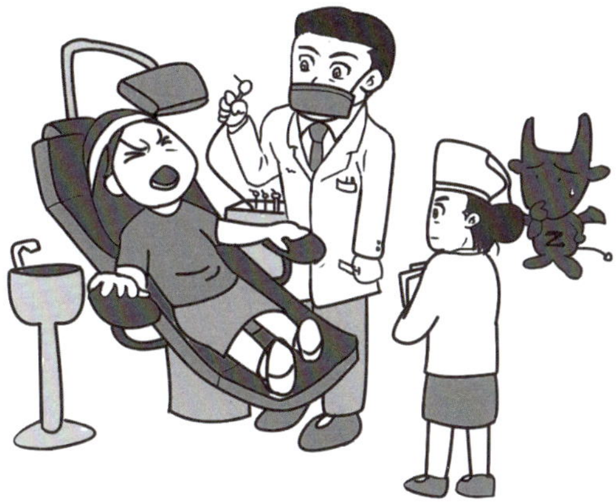

(A person is in a dentist's office with a dentist.)

Nurse	Sit down, please.
Mina	OK.
Doctor	Open your mouth.
Mina	Ahhh...
Doctor	(Lifts the drill for treatment)

(Mina makes a painful expression and Zeeto is watching.)

Pre-listening

T	Now, we're going to listen to the dialogue. Are you ready?
Ss	Yes (or Yes, we can).
T	Before listening to it, look at the book first. Open your book to page 38.
Ss	(Open their books.)

T	How do you feel about this picture? Can you guess what's going on in this picture?
Ss	Um...
T	Who do you see in this picture?
Ss	Mina, doctor...
T	Right. Mina, a doctor, and who else?
Ss	Nurse요!
T	Good! A nurse! Mina, a doctor, and a nurse. There are three people in this picture. Where are they?
Ss	Um...
T	Where are they? Where are Mina, a doctor and a nurse? A park? A bank? A school....?
Ss	Hospital요!
T	Wonderful! They are in a hospital. In more detail... Look at the picture again. Find some clues. Teeth...
Ss	Ah~ Den...dennnn
T	Denti...
S2	Ah, dentist!
Ss	Dentist! dentist!
T	Terrific! Dentist! Repeat after me. Dentist! Dentist! Mina is at a dentist's office with a dentist. What do you think they are doing?
Ss	Um.. (잘 못 알아듣는다.)
T	What are they doing? Are they dancing? Are they singing? Are they playing the piano?
Ss	Ah... Um... a doctor...
T	If you want, you can speak in Korean, too.
S1	의사선생님이 미나를 치료하고 계세요.
T	Right! The dentist is treating Mina. All right! Now let's watch the screen and listen to the dialogue together.

While-listening

	(The teacher shows the video clip without sound by clicking the play button on the background screen.)
T	This time I'll turn off the sound.
	(after watching) Can you guess what's going on? Where is Mina?
S3	Yes! Mina in the dentist's office!
T	Good! Mina is in the dentist's office. Anything else?
Ss	...
T	OK. This time let's watch the screen with sound. Please, try to catch any word in the dialogue. Right? OK, here we go.
	(Testing)
T	Can you hear it clearly?
Ss	너무 커요...웅웅거려요.
T	Let me turn it down a bit. Is it fine with you?
Ss	Yes.
	(Turn the volume down a bit and watch the screen.)

Post-listening

T	What words did you hear? Tell me any word you've heard.
S4	Mouth요!
T	Great! (point her mouth) Mouth! Repeat after me, mouth! mouth! mouth! Anything else?
S5	OK요! OK.
T	OK~ (students laugh) OK. Good~. That's right.
	Anything else?
Ss	Open, Open 요! you요!
	(Teacher write down what students said on the blackboard)

T	Open. Good! and.. you...? (your를 염두해 두지만 일단 학생이 말한대로 you로 쓴다)
S6	Sit down요.
T	Right! Sit down... (말끝을 흐리면서 학생들의 대답을 유도한다.)
S6	Please!!! Sit down please!
T	Brilliant! Sit down, please! Everybody did a great job! This time, please try to find how these words are put together in the dialogue while watching the video clip again. Got it? Here we go~! (Watching the video clip again) (A teacher and students ask and answer the 6 questions together in English.)
Q1	What have you heard? Try to find any word while listening.
Q2	Are there any new words?
Q3	Where did Mina go? / To the dentist's office.
Q4	What did the nurse say?/ Sit down, please.
Q5	What did the dentist say?/ Open your mouth.
Q6	When the dentist said, 'Open your mouth,' what did Mina do?

Questions for discussion

(1) Do you think the teacher does pre-listening activities well? If yes, what are the examples of pre-listening activities?

(2) How does the teacher manage the students who don't understand him/her in pre-listening activities?

(3) First, think of example tasks for while-listening. Do you think the teacher teaches while-listening activities well?

(4) What is the main task that the teacher does for post-listening activities?

2 Teaching Speaking

In regards to teaching speaking in primary English classrooms, we will look at the following questions:

1) Can you speak English? What does 'I can speak English' mean?
2) Are there any linguistic features of the spoken text that are different from the written text?
3) What are the unique characteristics of conversation?
4) How can teachers and students interact with each other in the classroom?
5) What are the models for teaching speaking in the classroom?
6) How can we teach speaking based on 'Presentation-Practice-Production'?
7) Is there any model procedure for teaching speaking in the classroom?

1. Do you speak English?

We often ask someone whether he/she can speak English or not as in the following example.

Ex) A: Do you speak English?
B: Yes, just a little.

In this conversation, what does B mean? Choose one of the following options.

- I can pronounce English words and sentences like English native speakers.
- I know many English words.
- I know English grammar well.
- I can carry on a conversation reasonably competently. (Brown, 2001, p. 267)

In order to speak English well, good pronunciation, knowledge of words and grammar seems necessary but are not the only conditions. Even though his/her pronunciation is poor, and he/she does not know English structure well, he/she can carry on a conversation well. The bottom line is how he/she makes himself/herself understood.

2. Linguistic features of the spoken text

Spoken language is the main focus of classroom interaction. But it is very difficult for us to follow the spoken text in that speakers use a lot of tactics to manage the interaction. Some of the features of the spoken text (Brown, 2001; Flowerdew & Miller, 2005; Hancock, 2003; Rost, 2002; Underwood, 1989) are:

- phonological contractions
  Ex) I'll ask her (like *Alaska*), We've seen him (like *wiv seen im*)
- hesitations, false starts, and filled pauses such as 'uh, um, well, you know, I mean, like, etc.'
- sentence fragments rather than complete sentences
  Ex) (Are you) coming (to dinner)?
- high incidence of questions and imperatives
- frequent use of first and second person pronouns

3. The features of conversations

Conversations are the most important among the spoken texts in classroom interaction. During the interaction, they negotiate meaning to the utterances using plenty of tactics. We will look at some features of conversations based on Flowerdew and Miller (2005, pp. 52~58) and Rost (2002, pp. 45~46).

1) Stages in the conversation

- Conversations can be broken down into three major stages: openings, closings, and topics. We should interact with one another appropriately at each stage.
- In opening a conversation, there must be an initiator, or speaker, but there must also be an interlocutor, or listener. And we can talk about greetings, weather, sports, etc.

A: How have you been? You look good.
B: Couldn't be better.

- In closing a conversation, the speaker says goodbye to the listener. Therefore, a listener's inability to pick up when the speaker is wanting to close the conversation can lead to an embarrassing situation like the following example.

A: Well, nice talking to you.
B: Yes, it's been lovely. We must do this again.
A: Well, I really must go now.
B: Where are you going?
A: Oh, I'm going to get some clothes at the department store.
B: That's nice. I'll come with you.
A: Oh, er . . . , I have to go to the bank first.

2) Turn-Taking

- Turn-taking means how interlocutors take turns at speaking and listening. The common rule for turn taking is that the person who speaks first becomes a listener, and then the listener takes his/her turn as a speaker.
- An example: a question is usually followed by an answer but can, in certain circumstances, …

A: What are you doing this weekend?
B: Do you have any plan?

3) Back-Channeling

- In order for speakers to continue with their message, they need signals, or *back-channel cues*, from their listeners to let the speakers know that they are paying attention.
- Back-channel cues may be verbal (*yeah, mm, um, ah, of course, oh dear, my God, etc.*) or nonverbal (head nodding, shoulder shrugging, facial gestures and eye contact, laughter, etc.).
- Appropriate back-channel cues facilitate a speaker to keep talking to a listener.

4) Repair

- Listeners may alter the direction by correcting misunderstandings, inaccuracies, or errors (repair). They can change an unfamiliar structure to a well-known one.

A: Do you mind if I open the window?
B: Yes.
A: Eh… I mean, may I open it?
B: Yes.

5) Reformulation

- A speaker initiates an utterance, so speaking is in the hands of a speaker. But, when the meaning is not clear, listeners can clarify for speakers how they are interpreting what is being said.

Patient: I can't make it tomorrow at 11:00 o'clock. I've got a lecture.
Doctor: Do you want to make the appointment a bit later?
Patient: Yes. How about 3:30?
(Doctor uses a paraphrase to reformulate what he/she understands the patient to have said.)

6) Topic shift

- In real life interaction, the listener may choose between continuing with the current topic or switching to a new one. The point is when is the appropriate time for a topic shift. The moment is not in the middle of the current topic but after concluding the topic.

A: I'd like this guide book, please.
(pause)
B: Here it is. (hands over the book)
A: Can I get some postcards?

4. Practices of classroom talk between the teacher and students

1) Informal talk with students

- The teacher talks to the students informally so as to break the ice before entering the main topic.

- The topics for informal talks are as follows: 'How's the weather?,' 'What day is it today?,' 'What happened to you?' etc.
- What are the benefits of informal talk with children?

Ex. 1)

T: You look so sad.
Aren't you well today?
S1: Not me. My mommy hospital.
T: Oh! Your mommy's in hospital. Why?

Ex. 2)

T: OK, let's check the roll. Now, remember to answer, 'I'm here.'
Jimin.
S1: I'm here.
T: Tim. (*silence*)
Ss: Not here.
T: What about Tim? Where is he?
Ss: I don't know.
T: OK, everyone's here except Tim.

Ex. 3)

T: How's the weather?
S: Raining.
T: It's raining hard.
I don't like rainy days. Do you like rainy days, Su-nam?
S1: Yes, I do.
T: Really? What do you usually do on rainy days?
S1: (No answer)
T: Play soccer? Ride a bike?
S1: Computer game.
T: OK. You like computer games.

Ex. 4)

T: Good morning. What's the name of the day today?
Is today Wednesday?

S: No.

T: Or maybe Tuesday? Or Sunday?

S1: No.

T: Oh I wish it was Sunday. OK, what day is it today?

S: Monday.

T: Great! Today is Monday.

2) Questions to elicit speaking

If teachers really like to interact with children, the level of your talk should be within their zone of proximal development space (ZPD). That is, your talk should not go beyond their linguistic ability. Most good teachers ask students questions according to their abilities like the following.

- Questions to elicit speaking (Slattery & Willis, 2001, p. 49)
  - Wh-question: *What's this*?
  - Questions using intonation only: *A dog*?↗
  - Questions using inversion: *Is this an elephant*?
  - Unfinished sentence questions with rising intonation: *This is a …*?↗
  - Either/or questions: *Is this an elephant or a kangaroo*?

Ex. 1) Either/or questions

T: What's this?
This is a …?

Ss: (Silent)

T: Lion? Tiger?

Ss: A cheetah.

T: Right! This is a cheetah.
And this is …?

S1: A mouse.

T: OK, this is a mouse.

Now, look at this picture. Is this a monkey or a kangaroo?

Ss: A monkey.

T: Right. This is a monkey.

OK, what's that? Is that a cat or a mouse?

Ss: A mouse.

T: Good. That is a mouse.

Ex. 2) (Describing a woman in the picture)

T: Is there a girl in this picture?

S: Yes.

T: Is there a boy in this picture?

S: No.

T: Is the girl happy or sad?

S: Happy.

T: Yes, she's happy, not sad.

S: Not sad.

T: Right, she's *not sad.* She's happy.

What is she wearing?

S: T-shirt.

T: Yes, she's wearing a T-shirt. What color is the T-shirt?

S: Red.

T: OK, she's wearing a red T-shirt. And what do you see behind her?

S: Pond.

T: Yes, there is a pond.

In the pond are there _______

S: Duck.

T: Right! There are ducks in the pond. (based on Krashen & Terrell, 1983, p. 79)

3) Negotiation of meaning in classroom talk

Once students are in the interaction with the teachers, then teachers should try to fill the gaps. Considering students' limited linguistic knowledge, teachers can invite students to the journey like the following:

- Students often use the structures already learned to new contexts like Ex. 1 to 4.

Ex. 1)

T: Who is the boy?
S: It's Jinho. (He's Jinho.)
T: Yes, he's Jinho.

Ex. 2)

S: (At the end of the class)
Where homework? (What is the homework?)
T: Not today. Tomorrow is Sports Day.
You have no homework.
What is the homework for today?
S: No homework.

Ex. 3)

S: I go Seoul.
T: You're going to Seoul?
S: [doesn't understand] What?
T: You will go to Seoul?
S: Yes.
T: When?
S: Last week.
T: Oh, you went to Seoul last week.
S: Yes. I go Seoul last week. (based on Brown, 2000, p. 228)

Ex. 4)

S: Many fish are in the lake.
These fish are serving in the restaurants near the lake.

T: [laughing] The fish are serving?

S: [laughing] Oh, no, the fish are served in the restaurant!

(Brown, 2000, p. 228)

- Teachers and students use comprehension checks, clarification requests, or paraphrases etc. to negotiate the meaning like Ex. 5 to 7.

Ex. 5)

T: Go down to the underground. Do you know the word underground?

S: I don't know.

T: Well, underground means the subway.

S: I see, underground.

Ex. 6)

T: First walk across the road, turn right and go straight two blocks ---

S: Did you say 'turn right'?

T: Yes.

Ex. 7)

T: I went to a Christmas Eve party.

S: Christmas Eve?

T: Right. December 24, the night before the Christmas.

S: I understand.

5. Models of teaching oral skills

1) Models of teaching speaking

(1) Presentation → Practice → Production (3P) (Harmer, 2001)

-Presentation: Teachers introduce a situation which contextualizes the new language, and then the language is presented.

-Practice: Students practice the language using accurate reproduction techniques.

-Production: Students are asked to use the new language in sentences of their own (immediate creativity).

Table 1. The 3P Teaching Cycle

(adapted from Nunan, 1999)

	Presentation	Practice	Production
Role of teacher	model	monitor	conductor
Role of students	listener	performer	interactor
Type of activity	lecture	drill	role play
Class organization	whole class	pairs	small group

(2) Johnson (1982)

- Follows 3P.
- The teacher can return to either presentation or practice when necessary after the production phase is over.

(3) Byrne (1986)

- Follows 3P.
- Joining the three phases in a circle. Teachers and students can decide at which stage to enter the procedure.

(4) Scrivener (1994): ARC

- Authentic use → Restricted use → Clarification and focus
- Authentic use: communicative activity
- Restricted use: drill, jazz chant, and elicited dialogue etc.
- Clarification and focus: Explaining grammar, giving examples, and analysing errors etc.
- 3P = CRA in this model

(5) Harmer (1998): ESA

- Engage: Unless students are engaged emotionally with what is going on, the learning will be less effective.
- Study: The focus is on how something is constructed: relative clauses, specific intonation patterns, the construction of a paragraph or text.
- Activate: Activating students' knowledge e.g. doing communicative activities
- ESA can also be EAS.

(6) Paul (2003)

Notice → Want → Challenge → Play → Succeed → Link

- Notice: "Huh? What's that?"
- Want: If the children are enjoying the activity they will want to find out what these new words and patterns mean.
- Challenge: Teachers can ask like this: "What is it? What's she doing? What's this in English?"
- Play: Doing a lot of activities
- Succeed: If the new language is at an achievable level, the children will be successful in understanding and using individual words and sentences.
- Link: The children are more likely to link it into the mental model.

6. Practices of teaching oral skills based on 3P

1) Presentation

Careful presentation can lead to good notice on the part of students. Teachers present the new learning items using the following various techniques (based on Ytreberg, 1990). The point is that students focus on what you are saying and they make plausible hypotheses on the target language items.

(1) Through students or famous persons

- *'Listen to me, please. Yuna can skate. Jimin can skate, too. Taehwan can swim. Sunjin can swim, too.'*

(2) Using class mascots or puppets

- Use class mascots or puppets as the teacher's interaction partner.
- Puppets can be uncomplicated like these examples: Sock puppets, stick puppets, paper bag puppets, finger puppets, etc.
- *T: Teddy, can you swim?*
  Teddy: No, I can't, but I can sing.
  (Teddy sings a song)
- *T: Sam, do you like basketball?*
  Sam: No, I don't.
  T: What about volleyball?
  Sam: Yes, I love it.

(3) Drawings

- Teachers can use very simple line drawings on the board.
- Ex) *What's he doing? (Drawing a person who is swimming) He is swimming.*

(4) Silhouettes

- Teachers sometimes use silhouettes to make children interested rather than clear pictures.
- You can use silhouettes on the overhead projectors; they can be given movement if you attach a piece of wire to them.

(5) Pictures

Ex 1) He used to be . . .

T: (*showing the thin man*) He's thin now. (*opening the flap and showing the overweight man*) But he used to be fat. (based on Wright, 1989, p. 37)

Ex 2) She's going to . . .

T: (*having folded the device and showing the first picture only*) What is she doing?
S: She's walking.
T: Good! She's walking toward the steps. What is she going to do? (*Still showing the first picture and asking the class to guess what she is going to do next.*)
S: She's going to climb the stairs.
T: Right! She's going to go up the stairs.
(*Now, show the picture in which the girl is going up the stairs*)
What's she doing now?
S: She's going up the stairs.
(based on Wright, 1989, pp. 34~35)

(6) Miming

- Teachers can mime using only parts of the body.
  · I walk. I jump. I write. I swim. I fly …
- Mime using realia (eg. clothes, telephones, animals, toy furniture, etc.)
  · Put a sweater on.
  · Kangaroos jump.

(7) Visual materials

- Teachers also can present new words or expressions with CDs or videos etc.

2) Practice

In the practice stage, students automatize the new learning items through controlled and guided practice.

(1) Controlled practice

The main emphasis is on the mechanical drill of the new learning items. But, when practicing the structures, accompany them with the related pictures or realia.

① Listen and repeat

- T: I'm going to the park.
  S: I'm going to the park.
  T: (Holding up a picture of a post office)
  S: I'm going to the post office.
  T: (Holding up a picture of an airport)
  S: I'm going to the airport.

② Substitution Drill

T: He's going to eat the cake.
S: He's going to eat the cake.
T: coffee.
S: ______________________________.
T: TV.
S: ______________________________.

③ Question & Answer

Ex. 1)

T: (Putting up a picture of a soccer field) Are you going to the soccer field?
T: Yes, I'm going to the soccer field. (Answering himself.)
T: (Putting up a picture of a park) Are you going to the park?
T: Yes, I'm going to the park. (Answering himself.)
T: (Putting up a picture of a library) Are you going to the library?
Ss: ______________________________.
T: Very good.
T: (Keeping asking two or three questions to students.)
S: (Answering questions immediately)
T: (Putting up a picture of a supermarket) Are you going to the bus station?
T: No, I'm going to the supermarket.
T: (Putting up a picture of a bookstore) Are you going to the bus station?
Ss: ______________________________.

T: Very good.

T: (Keeping asking two or three questions with negative answers to students. Then, putting up a picture of a post office) Are you going to the post office?

Ss: (Hesitating) ____________________________.

Ex. 2): Telling the time

S1: What time is it?

S2: (Looking at a clock) It's half past ten.

(S1, S2 know the time before they ask and answer about the time.)

Ex. 3): What's he/she doing?

S1: What's he doing?

S2: (Looking at a picture.) He's jumping.

(S1, S2 know what S2 is doing.)

Ex. 4): What do you do on Monday?

S1: What do you do on Monday?

S2: (Looking at the picture representing Monday's schedule)
I go to math class.

S1: What do you do on Tuesday?

S2: (Looking at the picture representing Tuesday's schedule)
I go to P.E. class.

Picture: 40 ÷ 5 = ???	Picture: Badminton
Monday	Tuesday
Picture: A: Where are you from? B: I am from Canada.	Picture: sketchbook, painting brush,
Wednesday	Thursday

(2) Guided practice

To encourage students to keep practicing, the practice itself should be interesting and meaningful to students. Then, through the active practice, students can learn the new structures automatically.

① Question / Answer

Ex. 1)

S1: What time is it?

S2: It's ____________ (Putting the clock to the time he likes and answers.)

② Questionnaires, Surveys, Time tables, etc.

If the contents of the surveys have personal significance to the students, students are eagerly engaged in the process and then learn the target structure.

Ex. 2)

Name	Fish	Apples	Spaghetti	Grapes	Bananas
철수	○	X	○	X	○
수미					
인호					
영미					

Sujin: Do you like fish?

Chulsu: Yes, I do.

Sujin: Do you like apples?

Chulsu: No, I don't.

Ex. 3) School timetable

S1: When do you have history class?

S2: History class. Let me see.
On Monday we have one history class.

S1: Really? What time is history class?

S2: At 11:45.

S1: OK. How about Tuesday?

S2: On Tuesday we don't have history class.

S1: How about Wednesday?

S2: On Wednesday we have two history classes.

S1: Good! When is history class?

S2: It starts at 9.

S1: Oh, I see.
Then, how about Thursday and Friday?

S2: We don't have any history classes on Thursday and Friday.

S1: Yes, you're right.

<table>
<tr><th></th><th>Monday</th><th>Tuesday</th><th>Wednesday</th><th>Thursday</th><th>Friday</th></tr>
<tr><td>9:00-9:45</td><td>Geography</td><td rowspan="2">Science</td><td rowspan="2">History</td><td>English</td><td rowspan="2">Math</td></tr>
<tr><td>9:45-10:30</td><td>English</td><td>Science</td></tr>
<tr><td></td><td colspan="5">Break</td></tr>
<tr><td>11:00~11:45</td><td>Math</td><td>English</td><td>Math</td><td>Geography</td><td>Science</td></tr>
<tr><td>11:45-12:30</td><td>History</td><td>Geography</td><td>Art</td><td>Music</td><td>English</td></tr>
<tr><td></td><td colspan="5">Lunch</td></tr>
<tr><td>2:00-2:45</td><td rowspan="2">Computer Studies</td><td rowspan="2">Social Studies</td><td rowspan="2">Art</td><td rowspan="2">Music</td><td rowspan="2">P.E.</td></tr>
<tr><td>2:45-3:30</td></tr>
</table>

③ Information gap activities

Ex. 4) What time is it in Seoul?

- Work with your partner.
- Give out a set of maps (MEST, 2009, p. 44 (4th grade) to pairs. One for Student A and the other for Student B.
- Each student asks and tells the time using 'What time is it in …?'
- Please don't look at your partner's map.

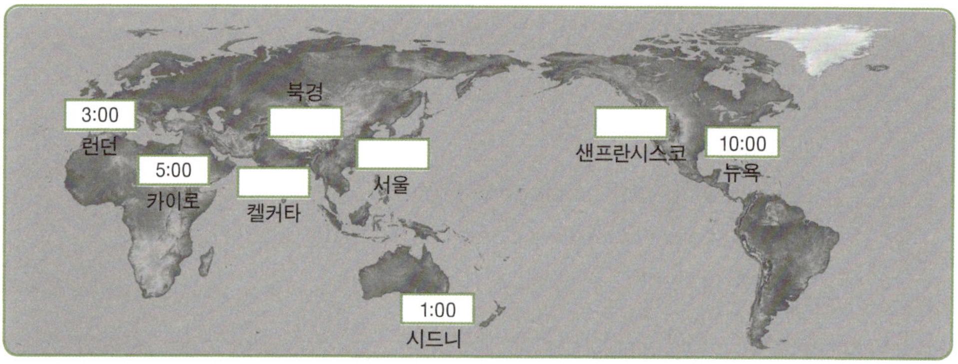

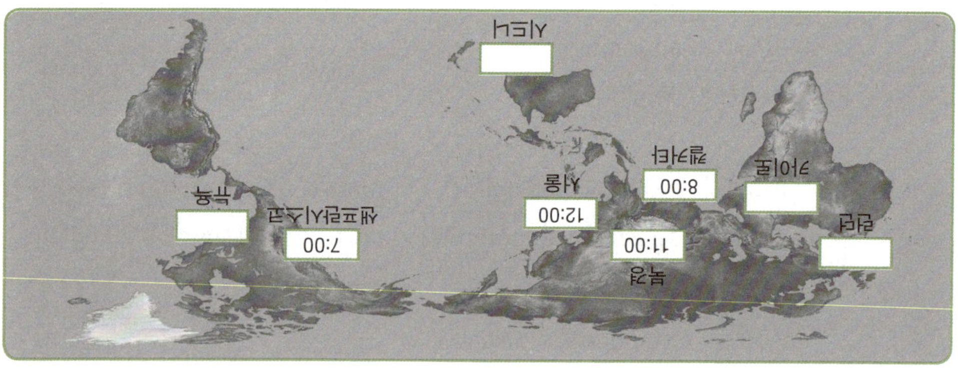

④ Guessing game

Ex. 5) Practicing 'What's this?' & 'It's …'

(Covering up an object with small pieces of paper)

T: (Removing a piece) What's this?

S1: I don't know.

T: (Removing one more piece) What's this?

S2: It's an elephant.

T: No, it isn't. (Removing one more piece) What's this?

S3: It's a tiger.

Ex. 6) Practicing 'What's he doing?' & 'He's ---ing.'

T: (showing a picture of a man jumping but covering up most of it with another card) What's he doing?

S1: He's walking.

T: Is he walking?

S2: He's running

T: (moving down the card so that more can be seen) Is he running?

Ss: No, he isn't. He's jumping.

(based on Wright, 1989, p. 19)

3) Production

(1) Describing pictures (based on Ur, 1996)

- Make groups of 5 students, and decide on a secretary for each group.

- Give out a picture and a piece of paper with sentences which describe it.
- Each student describes the picture by turns, and the secretary puts a tick beside each sentence when it is used and who used it on the piece of paper.
- The student who has the most ticks wins the game.
- They repeat the game with other pictures.
- Reshuffle the teams including the position of secretary.

(2) Finding differences

- The students are in pairs; each member of the pair has a different picture. Without showing each other their pictures, they have to find out what the differences are between them.

- Find four differences (Example: based on Slattery & Willis, 2001)
  · Teacher: Work with your partner. I'll give out a pair of pictures to each pair. One for the first student, and the other for the second student. OK, so please don't show your pictures to your partner.
  · Teacher: OK, everybody. Look at only your picture. There are four differences in the pictures. So please talk about the picture and find out what the four differences are. OK?

  Sujin: A boy is riding a bicycle.
  Jimin: No. A boy is playing soccer.
  Sujin: A girl is flying a kite.
  Jimin: No. A girl is sitting on the grass.
  Sujin: A woman is reading a book.
  Jimin: Yes. A man is drawing a picture.

(3) Finding things in common (based on Ur, 1996)

- Walk around the classroom and choose a student who you don't know well. He/she is your partner.
- Talk to each other so that you can to find out as many things as possible that you have in common.

- Please find out things through talking only.
- At the end report your findings to the class.

7. Practice of teaching speaking in the primary classroom

How do primary English teachers teach speaking in their classrooms? We will see an example in the following. Ms. Choi teaches 'Look and Speak' of 'Lesson 5. May I help you? (MEST, 2009, p. 42 (Elementary school English 6))' to sixth graders.

Dialog 1

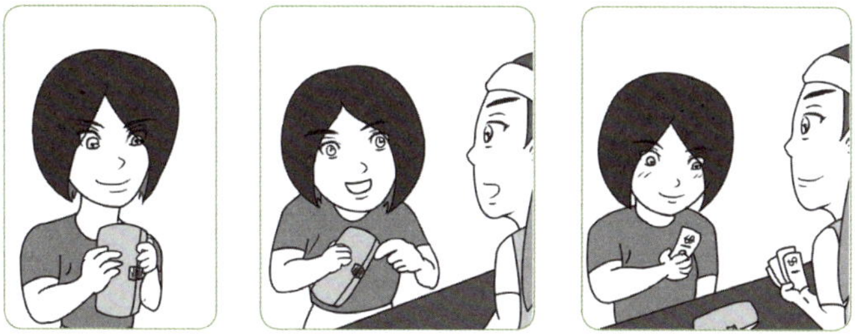

(Peter is looking for a pencil case at the stationery store.)

Peter (Approaching the clerk)
Excuse me.

Clerk May I help you?

Peter Yes, please.
How much is this pencil case?

Clerk It's $6.

Peter OK. I'll take it. (Handing $10 to the clerk.) Here your are.

Clerk (Counting the change and handing the change to Peter)
Here's your change. Thank you.

Pre-speaking

T Let's look at the pictures and guess what's happening.
Where is Peter in the first picture?

Ss He's at the 문구점.

T You're right. He's at the stationery store.
What's he looking for?

Ss I don't know.

T Come on!
What does he want to get?
Pencils? Notebooks?

Ss Colored pencils? Pencil case?

T Good guess!
What's happening in the second picture?
Who is the man?

Ss Clerk.

T Very good. He is a clerk.
What does the clerk say to Peter?

Ss "뭐가 필요하니?"

T Good! He says, "Can I help you?"
And, what does Peter say to the clerk?

Ss "How much ---?"

T You're right.
He says, "How much is this ---?"
Now, look at the last picture.
What does the clerk do?

Ss "거스름돈을 주고 있어요."

T That's right.
He's giving some change to Peter.
What does the clerk say?

Ss "Change ---."

T	Right.
	"Here's your change."
Ss	(Students says, "Here's your change.")
T	Very good!

While-speaking

T	Now, let's watch the CD-ROM and listen to the dialogue.
Ss	Yes, ma'am.
	(After watching the CD-ROM)
T	Look at the first scene! Peter is at the stationery story.
	What's he looking for?
Ss	Pencil case.
T	Right! He's looking for a pencil case.
	Now, look at the second scene.
	He comes to the clerk.
	What does Peter say?
Ss	"Excuse me."
T	Very good!
	He says, "Excuse me."
	And, what does the clerk say to Peter?"
Ss	"May I help you?"
T	Right. He says, "May I help you?" or "Can I help you?"
Ss	(Students say, "Can I help you?")
T	Good!
	Peter needs the pencil case.
	What does Peter say?
Ss	"I need the pencil case."
Ss	"How much is this pencil case?"

Ss	"I need the pencil case. How much is this?"
T	Well done! "How much is this pencil case?"
Ss	$6.
T	That's right. It's $6. What does Peter say?
Ss	"I'll take it."
T	Very good! He says, "I'll take it." And, says what?
Ss	"Here you are."
T	Terrific! Peter is handing a ten dollar bill to the clerk. Now, look at the last scene. What's the clerk doing?
Ss	He's handing the change to Peter.
T	Well done! The clerk says, "Here's your change."

Post-speaking

T	Now, can you buy things at the stationery store?
Ss	Of course.
T	Good! Now, let's play a mini game.
Ss	Wow!
T	Let's pretend we're at the stationery store. Each group needs a thing. And, I'm a clerk.
Ss	(Each group thinks of a thing to buy.)
T	Are you ready to start? Group 1?
Ss	Sure, we're ready.
T	Very good! Here we go!
G1	"Excuse me."
T	"May I help you?"

G1	"Yes, please." "How much is this notebook?"
T	"It's $7."
G1	"OK. I'll take it." (Handing $7 to the clerk.)
T	"Thank you."
T	Wonderful! Let's give a big hand to Group 1.

Questions for discussion

(1) Some students answer the teacher's questions in Korean. What do you think about such students' communications strategy in the classroom?

(2) How does the teacher give positive feedback to students' response?

(3) How does the teacher and students practice today's learning points in post-speaking activities?

3 Teaching Reading

In this chapter, we examine the following questions regarding teaching reading in primary English classrooms:

1) Through which processes do we reach reading comprehension?
2) What approaches can we use to teach reading to primary students?
3) What difficulties do we need to cope with when reading the text?
4) What are the main steps for teaching reading in the classroom?
5) What tasks for reading can be used in primary classrooms?
6) Is there any model procedure for teaching reading in the classroom?

1. The process of reading comprehension

What is reading? How can readers perceive a written text in order to understand its meaning? Among bottom-up processing, top-down processing, and interactive processing, many second language researchers view interactive processing as the most persuasive. Using this processing, an individual reader constructs meaning through a transaction with written text. The transaction involves the reader's interpreting the text, based on the reader's past experiences, language background, and cultural framework, as well as the reader's purpose for reading (Hudelson, 1994, p. 130).

Then, what kinds of knowledge are involved in the processing? According to Grabe (1991, p. 379), six general component skills and knowledge types are needed for reading comprehension:

1) Automatic recognition skills - a virtually unconscious ability, ideally requiring little mental processing to recognize text, especially word identification.
2) Vocabulary and structural knowledge - a sound understanding of language structure and a large recognition vocabulary
3) Formal discourse structure knowledge - an understanding of how texts are organized and how information is put together into various genres of text.
4) Content/world background knowledge- prior knowledge of text-related information and a shared understanding of the cultural information involved in text.
5) Synthesis and evaluation skills/strategies- the ability to read and compare information from multiple sources, to think critically about what one reads, and to decide what information is relevant or useful for one's purpose.
6) Metacognitive knowledge and skills - monitoring an awareness of one's mental processes and the ability to reflect on what one is doing.

2. Approaches to teaching second language reading

Learning to read can begin from text level; from sentence level; from word level; from letter level. Each starting point has produced approaches to teaching reading that can be used in the foreign language classroom such as 'phonics teaching,' 'language experience approach,' 'flash cards,' and 'emergent literacy' (Cameron, 2001; Nation, 2009; Scott & Ytreberg, 1990).

1) Phonics teaching

- Phonics teaching tries to teach reading from the bottom-up. It emphasizes matching individual letters to their sounds.

- If phonics teaching works well, it helps children make mental connections between letters and sounds. As a result, students can read the words of any text even though they do not know what it means.
- Progression in phonics teaching (Ediger, 2001, p. 157)
  Although phonics approaches vary, the usual way proceeds from consonants to vowels and from single letters to combined letters in approximately the following order:

Consonants(C)

① For which there is a single sound: 'b, d, f, j, k, l, m, n, p, r, s, t, v, z'

② For which there is more than one sound: 'c' in 'cat' / 'c' in 'city,' 'g' in 'gas' / 'g' in 'gem'

③ Which occur in two-letter combinations, or 'blends'
with l: bl, cl, fl, gl, pl, sl
with r: br, cr, dr, fr, gr, pr, tr
with s: sc, sk, sm, sn, sp, st, sw

④ Which occur in three-letter blends: scr, spr, str, squ

⑤ Which combine to form a new sound, or digraph: 'ch, sh, th, wh, gh, nk, ng'

Vovels (V)

⑥ Long vowels

CV	be
CVe	ate, like, rote
CVVC	paid, boat

⑦ Short vowels

VC or CVC	it, hot

⑧ r-controlled vowels

Vr or CVr	art, car, her

⑨ digraph/diphthong

VV	saw, book; boil, out

2) Language experience approach

- The language experience approach starts children reading and writing at sentence level, and its key feature is the child's use of his / her own experiences or interests as the topic of texts.
- Procedure:
  (1) Each child draws a picture or tells a story that recently happened to him/ her or something that they are very interested in: e.g. 'I went to Everland yesterday.'
  (2) Children compose sentences with the help of the teacher. They can use words cards to make the sentences, if possible.
  (3) The sentence is then read back to the teacher, and the child copies it down in her or his book.
  (4) The child practices reading it, and reads it to the class, and family.
  (5) These pictures and texts, all written by the child, are gathered together, and are a personal reading book for that learner.

3) Flash cards

- This approach starts from word level, with children looking at single words on cards called 'flash cards', because they are sometimes shown very quickly to the children to encourage rapid whole word recognition.
- Procedure:
  (1) The teacher shows a word among the words already orally produced. Sometimes flash cards are shown very quickly to help the children to recognize the words automatically.
  (2) And then, the teacher reads the word pointing to the object.
  (3) Children repeat after the teacher and keep practicing.
  (4) Finally, children try to read the books that are tuned to their reading abilities.

4) Emergent literacy

- 'Emergent literacy' describes the first language phenomenon in which children seem to learn to read without any teaching, gradually, and through exposure to text and to reading (Hall, 1987).
- Procedure:
  (1) Children choose the books they want to hear and read.
  (2) Parents can read aloud the books to children.
  (3) Some will begin to work out for themselves the patterns that link spoken and written text.
  (4) Emergent readers often begin to know by heart sentences from favorite books. They learn the sentences from hearing them again and again, and will say them along with the books.
- Emergent literacy ideas may have potential in primary classrooms, but in order for literacy to emerge, the following conditions are needed: 1) a skilled and qualified teacher, 2) various children's story books which are interesting and appropriate, and 3) accompanying formal teaching.

3. Reading strategy

When we read, we can not understand all of the words or expressions. In these cases, we can use lots of strategies to make up for the lack of knowledge. For a better reader, it is indispensable for you to be well-trained with the following reading strategies. Before you start to read, identify what your purpose for reading is. It directs you to follow a specific track. That is, the ways you read depend on your purposes as in the following (based on Brewster, Ellis, & Girard, 1991; Brown, 2001):

(1) Reading for fun or pleasure: When you read interesting cartoons or stories, you disregard the details including unknown words and expressions and keep reading to the end. Therefore, you enjoy reading and do not stop.

(2) Skimming: When you want to know the topic or the purpose of the text quickly, you do not have to read the whole sentences from the first to the end. You can skip the less important words and sentences and follow the meaning.

(3) Scanning: Let us suppose you are looking at the train table and you want to know the earliest train for Seoul around three in the afternoon. In this case, you do not have to look at the table from the top to the end. You can just look at the table around three p.m.

(4) Phonics: When you come across unknown words, use phonics rules to try to pronounce the words. Reading aloud the words is the first step to reading and then you can struggle to match the sounds to the meanings.

(5) Guessing: It is a good strategy when you tackle the meanings of the unknown words and their grammatical relationships. Use sight words, pictures in the book, or background knowledge related to the text.

(6) Semantic mapping: In order to understand the text well, build semantic mapping for a key word through brainstorming with your partners. The flows of the concepts like this can be a good guiding light and then you can read the text well.

(7) Text organization: So as to read the text fast, find the organization of the texts such as 'listing, time order, cause-effect and comparison-contrast.' To identify the text organizations, first look for the key words, topics, or main ideas of the texts.

4. How does the teacher teach reading in the classroom?

What are useful steps for teaching reading in the classroom? Like teaching other language skills, when teachers teach reading, they often follow the procedure of pre-reading, while-reading and post-reading activities. We will examine these steps using the following example.

This is a horse.
He is happy.

1) Pre-reading activity

- Guess what the reading is about.

T: What is this?
S: It's a horse.
T: That's right. It's a horse.
Can you find the word 'horse'?
S: Sure.
T: Good!
(Showing the word 'lion.') Horse?
S: No, lion.
T: Very good. (Showing the word 'horse.') Horse?
S: Yes, horse.
T: You're right. (Putting the word 'horse' next to the picture 'horse.') Horse.
(Showing the word 'sad') Is the horse sad?
S: No, happy.
T: Right. He's not sad. (Putting the word 'happy' next to the picture 'horse') He's happy.

2) While-reading activity

- Read the sentences while pointing to the words next to the pictures.
- The teacher reads some words and asks students to point to them.
- Students point to the sentence that the teacher has read.
- The teacher starts reading first and stops to invite students to try to read some words.

  T: This is a . . .

  S: Horse.

  T: He is . . .

  S: Happy.

  T: That's right. This is a horse. He is happy.
- Listen and read each sentence after the teacher.

3) Post-reading activity

- Draw a picture of friends, family members, etc. And write either words or sentences.
  · S1: This is my dad. He is tired.
  · S2: Changho. Happy.
  · S3: . . . . . .

5. Tasks for teaching reading

The Korean alphabet is different from that of the English language. Therefore it needs careful and systematic instruction for reading in the primary classroom. Based on the National Curriculum, teachers must teach students how to read the alphabet letters, simple words and phrases, simple sentences and simple texts.

1) Reading the alphabet letters

(1) Reading the capital/ small letters

- Look and read the alphabet letters after the teacher.
- Point to the alphabet letters in the classroom that the teacher says.
- Give out the alphabet letters to each student. Show the alphabet card as the teacher says that letter.
  · Give out one alphabet letter to each student. Point to the child who has the alphabet letter that the teacher says.
- Find the letters that the teacher reads and color them.
- Find the same letter on the left and circle it. Letters are written on paper rolls, pens, candies, chocolates, fish, or tops.
  · Read the letter(s) on the left and find the same letter(s) on the right and circle them.

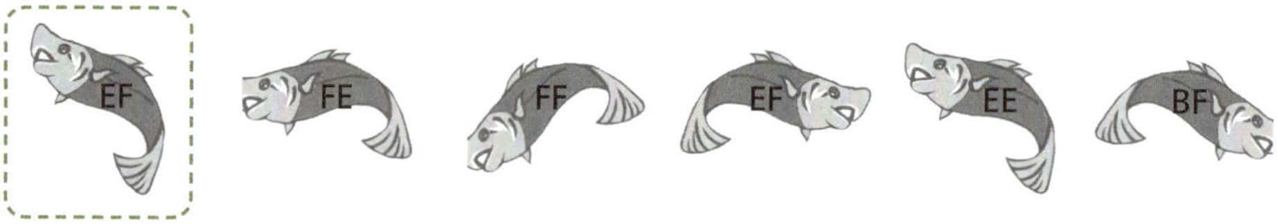

· Read the letter on the left and find the same letter in the words on the right and circle them.

- Find and read the alphabet letters in the words

  Ex 1)

K k

King

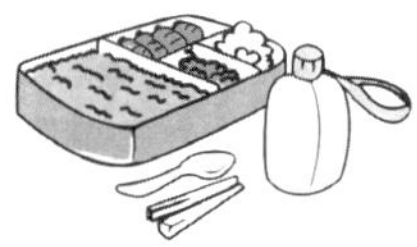

L l

Lunch

  Ex 2)

b

banana

book

baseball

bag

- Read the alphabet letters on the signs of public buildings or stores.

(2) Understanding the order of the alphabet

- Point and read aloud the alphabet letters from 'A/a to Z/z' as the teacher reads.
- Read the alphabet letters silently in the order of 'A/a to Z/z' and connect the dots.

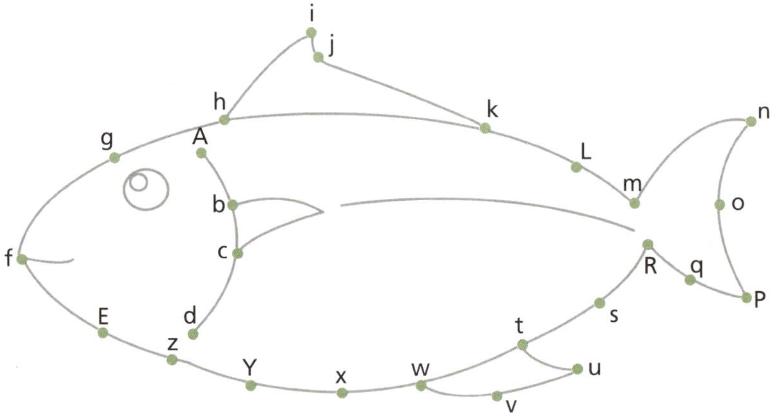

- Sing the alphabet song.

2) Reading the words

(1) Reading words aloud

- Read aloud words using pictures.

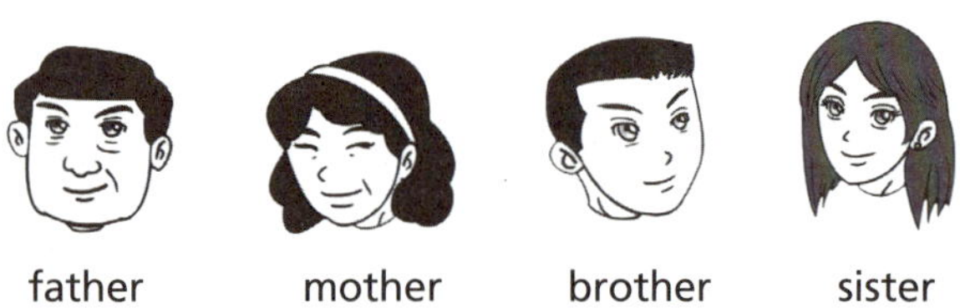

- Ex 1) Reading the words on objects, signs, or advertisements

- Ex 2) Reading the words related to family relationships used in the family tree

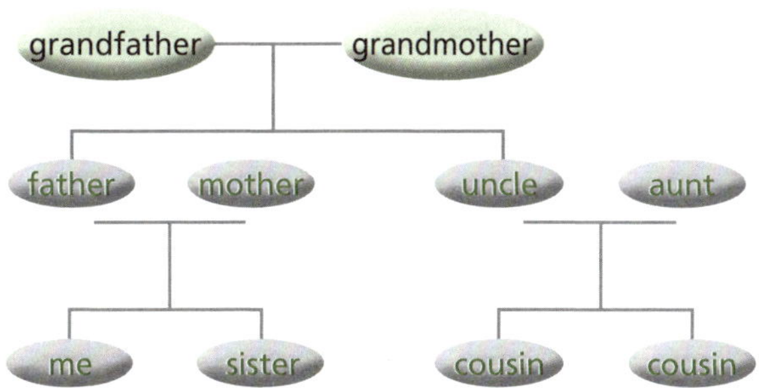

- Ex 3) Reading the words related to the emotions using the pictures

(2) Matching words to pictures

- Connect words to pictures and read them aloud.

girl book king

- Go down the ladder. If the word matches the picture, circle them. If they don't, make crosses.

house　　lion　　table　　nurse

- Connect the floors of the school to the words and read them aloud.

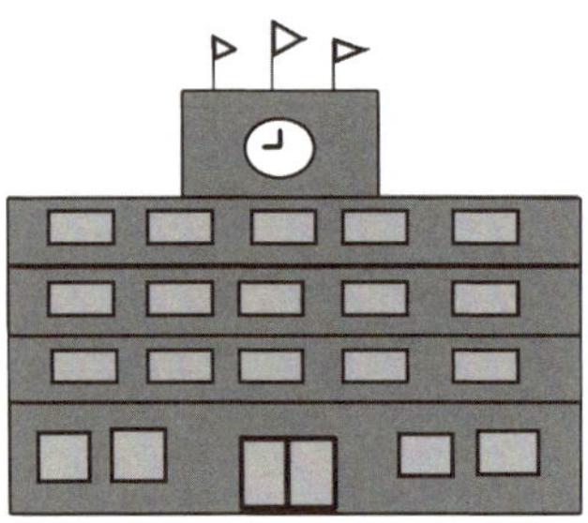

School

fourth floor
second floor
first floor
third floor

(3) Word search

B	T	E	N	N	I	S	E	N	N
A	A	M	Y	U	K	O	P	A	S
S	L	B	D	L	P	C	L	F	B
K	S	V	J	M	Z	C	I	Q	P
E	R	N	B	V	C	E	U	W	O
T	I	O	H	N	X	R	D	F	G
B	A	S	E	B	A	L	L	A	S
A	C	J	F	D	Z	S	W	E	M
L	E	U	G	E	A	T	Y	K	A
L	D	P	H	W	Q	J	R	T	R

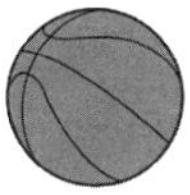

- Ex 1) Find the words in the 'Word Box.'
  - · Find the word using the picture with the word.
  - · Find the word using the picture.
  - · Find the word without using the picture.

- Ex 2) Find the words in the 'word train.' The 'word search' can be also shaped as snakes, kite tails, tree rings etc.

(4) Reading the words in the word puzzle

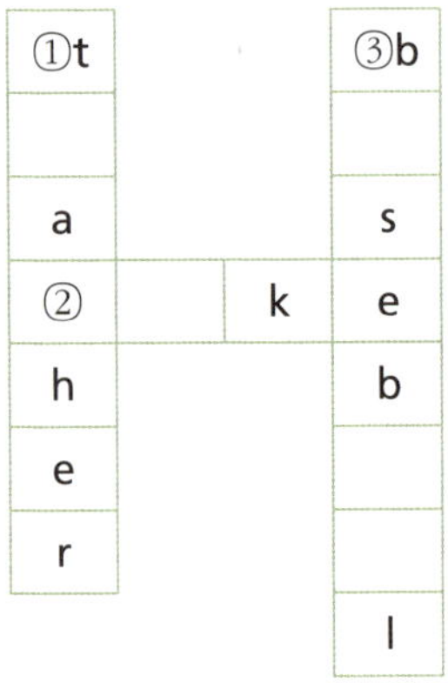

- Students can solve the puzzle using pictures or pictures with the word cues.

(5) Connecting words to related ones

① Find the similar words

· Find the words with similar pronunciation: (wear/pear, sun/fun).

· Connect the capital letter word to the small letter word.

② Find the opposite words

· hot/cold, summer/winter, tall/short

③ Odd one out

· Find the one that does not fit.

Ex) doctor - scientist - piano - singer

④ Connecting the verbs to the nouns

Ex 1)	watch •		• TV
	eat •		• juice
	drink •		• pizza
Ex 2)	see •		• ears
	smell •		• eyes
	hear •		• nose

(6) Simple word games

① Card matching game

· The teacher points to a picture card, then students show the matching word card, and read the word.

· In group work, a student shows a picture card. The others find the matching word card and read the word.

· The teacher puts a word card next to a picture card. If they match, read the word. If they do not match, do not read. Correct the word.

② Speed game

· In group work, a student shows a picture, the others touch the matching word card as fast as possible. Or, put an eraser on the card quickly.

③ Guessing game

· Put word cards in the box.

· One student picks a card, and the others guess the card.

· Students take turns. The best guesser is the winner.

3) Reading the sentences

When we teach students to read a sentence, we had better use the words and phrases already learned. Also, the sentences are based on their experiences or interests.

(1) Reading aloud the sentences using the pictures

- Read aloud the sentences using the pictures.
- Read aloud the sentences with the help of the pictures with the key words.

(2) Connecting the sentences to the right pictures

- Read a sentence carefully and show the correct picture.
- Listen to the sentence carefully and find the correct picture.
- Listen to the sentences on the left and connect them to the correct pictures on the right.
- Match the road signs to the correct sentences.

1. Don't leave your car here.
2. Don't ride a bike here.

(3) Reading sentences using pictures in the sentences

- Without cues:

· Ex 1) Birds fly in the __________.

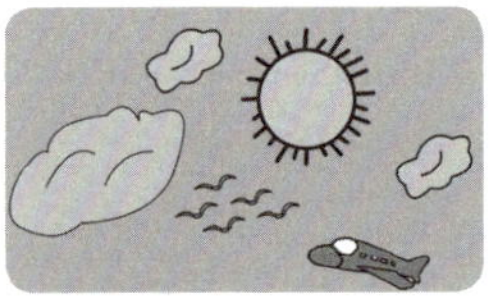

· Ex 2) Tom is ____________.

- With cues:

· Find the correct word for the picture in the 'example' and read the sentences.

Example: teacher, nurse, police officer, bank, post office, hospital

A: Where's the (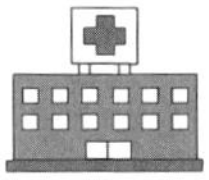) ?

B: I'm sorry, but you can ask a ().

(4) Making sentences out of words

- Arrange the words and make the sentences.
  - · A group comes to the front. Each student gets a word card. They arrange the words and make a sentence. Then, show the sentence to the class reading the sentence aloud.

- Make new sentences using the cues.
  - · Teacher shows a word card. Each group makes a sentence.

  Ex) T: (Present the word card 'fly.')

  G1: Birds fly.

(5) Simple sentence reading games

- Sentence reading board game
  - · Prepare a sentence board.
  - · Play the board game. The students must read the sentence correctly. Monitor carefully what they are reading.

- Making sentences by touching the word cards
  - · In pair work, a student says a sentence. The other one touches the word card in the same order that the first student has said.

4) Reading the simple text

It is very difficult for teachers to help children to understand the text. But, they are interested in reading the texts related to their experiences. Some of the examples are simple letters, personal diaries, daily routines, hobbies, invitation cards, introductions of themselves, family, or friends etc. The texts should be interesting so that children want to read them over and over again.

(1) Reading the text using pictures

- Read the text for fun using pictures.
- Read and try to understand the meaning of the text using the pictures and the key words.

(2) Finding topics or main ideas

- Find the correct picture to show an appropriate topic.
- Find the key idea among the choices.
- Choose the main idea among the underlined parts in the text.
- Write in short what the story is about.

(3) Understanding the details

- Answer the Y/N questions.
- Read the dialogue and find a picture that is not true.
- Connect the days of the week to the work to make it appropriate to the dialogue.
- Find the picture of what she did yesterday in the park.
- Find the picture where the dialogue is taking place.
- Read carefully and mark the thing that the boy is going to do.

(4) Completing the text

- Unscramble the sentences and complete the dialogue.
- Listen to the diary and arrange the sentences in the order of what happened.

- Match the pictures of his daily routine to their sentences and write his daily routine.

(5) Drawing a picture

- Complete the unfinished picture to match the text.
- Make a circle around the place that the boy is looking for.
- Follow the road in the order of the directions and find the route on the city map.

6. Practice of teaching reading in the primary classroom

How do primary English teachers teach reading in their classrooms? We will see an example in the following. Mr. Kim teaches 'Let's Read' of 'Lesson 7. My father is a pilot (MEST, 2009, p. 59 (elementary school English 6))' to sixth graders.

Script

This is my family.
My grandfather is a police officer.
My father is a nurse.
My mother is a pilot.

Before-reading

T	It's time to read! Can you see the TV clearly from the back seats?
Ss	Yes/ Yes, we can.
T	Open your book to page 59. Before reading it, look at the picture first. There's the same picture as on the TV.
Ss	(Open their books)
T	What do you think about this picture? Can you guess what's going on in this picture?
Ss	Um.. .
T	Who do you see in this picture?
Ss	Policeman, doctor, pianist, cook..
T	Right. Policeman or police officer, doctor, pianist, cook and who else?
Ss	Pilot, nurse!
T	Great! Pilot, nurse! And.. Nami! What do you think Nami is doing? Can you guess?
Ss	Um... 소개하는 것 같아요. 가족소개해요..
T	Nice guess! Anything else? All right! Let's check it together.
Ss	OK.
T	Can you read the sentences?
Ss	Um.. . (Some students read but some can not.)
T	Let's try it again slowly. (The teacher gives students some time to read the sentences by themselves.)

While-reading

T All right. Now let's watch the screen and listen to the sentences carefully.

(Click the sentences in the CD-ROM)

T There are four sentences in your book. We'll read the key words first.

Look at my lips. Repeat after me three times.

(family, family, family)

(a police officer, a police officer, a police officer.)

(a nurse, a nurse, a nurse.)

(a pilot, a pilot, a pilot.)

Ss (Ss repeat after the teacher.)

T Great! This time, let's read like the example.

(This/ is/ my family.

My grandfather/ is/ a police officer.

My father/ is/ a nurse.

My mother/ is/ a pilot.)

Ss (Ss repeat after the teacher.)

T Now, put them together. Repeat after me.

(This is my family.

My grandfather is a police officer.

My father is a nurse.

My mother is a pilot.)

Ss (Ss repeat after the teacher.)

T Terrific! Let's repeat after the CD-ROM.

Look at the first one. Listen carefully and repeat after them.

(Have Ss repeat after the CD-ROM using the exact pronunciation.)

(Have Ss read it individually.)

Post-reading

T	This time, you'll be the reader. This is pair work.
	One of you reads the sentence. The other listens to your partner and expresses the job with body language.
	(The teacher shows one example.)
T	Have you got it?
Ss	Yes!
T	The winner is the one who reads the sentence clearly and loudly.
Ss	OK. Yes!
	(Do the activity.)
T	Good! Now let's check it together!
	Are there any volunteers?
Ss	(Have two volunteers present what they have done.)
T	Excellent!
	(Have two more volunteers present what they have done.)
	Beautiful! You all did a great job.
	Let's read the sentences aloud.

Questions for discussion

(1) Do you think the teacher's presentation of the pre-reading activities is good? What are the examples of pre-reading activities given?

(2) What is the main while-reading activity? Do you think it is suitable for sentence level reading?

(3) What do students do for the post-reading activity? Do you think it facilitates students' participation in class?

4 Teaching Writing

Concerning teaching writing in primary English classrooms, we will try to solve the following questions:

1) Why do teachers teach writing to children?
2) What are the main features of teaching writing that is different from those of oral language teaching?
3) What are helpful tips to the teachers for teaching writing?
4) Are there any useful methods for teaching writing in the classroom?
5) What are the tasks for teaching writing that can be used in the primary classroom?
6) Is there any model procedure for teaching writing in the classroom?

1. Needs for teaching writing

Writing skills are considered the least important among the four language skills. And it takes a lot of time to master writing even for English native speakers. But writing is indispensable for communication through written language. One piece of good news for writing teachers is that children are highly motivated in writing. Let us have a closer look at the need for teaching writing in the primary classroom based on Byrne (1988, pp. 129~130).

① Children usually enjoy writing.
② Most children expect to be taught to write.
③ Children, like older students, need a break from oral work.
④ Writing gives children an opportunity to work at their own pace, which is very relaxing for them.
⑤ Access to the written language sometimes clears up difficulties which children have when learning orally.
⑥ Writing activities provide an opportunity for personal contact.
⑦ Children like and need to have a record of many of the things they do in the classroom - of dialogues they have practised and songs they have sung.
⑧ Children need the extra language contact that writing can provide, especially through some sort of homework activity.
⑨ Children need something to show their parents.

As we see above, children are interested in writing related to their school and personal life. What are examples of real life writing? What do children like to write the most?

① Note-taking in class
② Exchanging short notes with friends
③ Taking telephone messages
④ Keeping a diary
⑤ Writing letters / invitations / cards
⑥ Sending text messages
⑦ Writing reports on project work
⑧ Writing simple poems
⑨ Writing 'compositions' or stories.

2. Characteristics of teaching writing

Teaching writing and reading is different from teaching listening and speaking in that listening and speaking are using the spoken language, not the written language. And teaching writing aims at teaching a productive skill contrary to teaching reading. That is, when you teach writing to children, you can not use the advantages of spoken interaction. In the following, we examine the characteristics of teaching writing in the primary classroom (based on Scott & Ytreberg, 1990):

(1) First, when children communicate to others through writing, they can not utilize the characteristics of the non-verbal language such as body language, intonation, facial expressions, etc. Therefore students should write clearly in order not to be misunderstood.
(2) Second, it takes lots of time for children to master writing skills. Therefore, it needs various and systematic writing activities from controlled through guided to free writing focused on students' interests and experiences.
(3) Third, during meaningful writing activities, teachers do not correct students' minor language errors in order for children to keep writing.
(4) Finally, writing is a useful integrative activity for developing the language consciously different from spoken language skills.

3. Guidelines for teaching primary writing

As we have seen before, primary writing class is different from that of middle and high schools. Therefore, in order to teach primary writing to children successfully, you should ponder on 'guidelines for teaching primary writing' (based on Byrne, 1988, pp. 130~131).:

① Give the students plenty of opportunities for copying, e.g. lists of words, copies of songs, poems and dialogues.

② Give the students adequate opportunities to use orally learned language in writing.
③ Provide activities which the students can do at their own speed.
④ Work with the students whenever possible.
⑤ Make sure that the students begin to see writing as a means of communication.
⑥ Encourage the students to be creative.
⑦ Make writing activities enjoyable.

4. Types of primary classroom writing

What is the aim of classroom writing? Of course, it is free writing. The point is how teachers can help students write freely. According to the results of researchers (Brown, 2001; Rivers, 1981; Scott & Ytreberg, 1990), the types of primary classroom writing are as follows:

1) Copying

(1) Direct copying

- Copy directly what was produced orally or already read.
- Copy the words or sentences focusing on the sound-letter correspondence.
- The teacher can also describe students' drawings and then students copy the sentences.

(2) Matching and copying

- Instead of forcing students to copy any sentences, in 'matching', students can choose the sentence to copy.
- As a variation of direct copying, students can find a matching word or sentence to the given picture and then copy the sentence:

Ex.)

1. He is playing basketball.
2. He likes basketball.
3. He can play basketball well.
4. He is going to be a good basketball player.

(3) Arranging and copying

- Complete the blanked text using the given sentences, and then copy the whole text.
- The following example is to arrange the scrambled sentences and then complete the following letter:
  - · We went to Haeundae beach.
  - · It has beautiful beaches.
  - · We enjoyed delicious seafood there.
  - · Then we went to a restaurant.
  - · We're going to visit the famous aquarium.
  - · The water is blue and warm.

Dear John,

Pusan is fantastic. ______________________________

____

Yesterday ______________________________

____

Tomorrow ______________________________

Love, Su-mi

(4) Delayed copying

- Ask students to look at familiar words or sentences on the board for a few seconds.
- Erase the words or sentences and then ask students to write them.
- You can present the words or sentences using the monitor rather than the board.

(5) Copying notebook

- Encourage students to copy the words or sentences orally produced or already read spontaneously.
- Or, students can copy the words or sentences meaningful to them to be posted on the notice board.

2) Controlled writing

In controlled writing, students are required to reproduce the sentences with adaptations, which are already heard, produced orally and read in the books. This intensive writing typically appears in controlled, written grammar exercises. Of course, this type of writing does not allow for creativity on the part of the students.

An example of controlled writing is to change all present tense verbs to past tense. And another example is to change all the first person singular pronouns to the third person.

3) Guided writing

Students will be given more freedom in the selection of lexical items and structural patterns for their written exercises. This writing is also closely related with what they have read or heard.

- Writing summaries of stories they have studied in class
- Rewriting a dialogue in a narrative form
- A dicto-comp: First, a paragraph is read at normal speed, usually two or three

times; then the teacher asks students to rewrite the paragraph to the best of their recollection of the reading. In one of several variations of the dicto-comp technique, the teacher, after reading the passage, puts key words from the paragraph, in sequence, on the board as cues for the students.

4) Free writing

- Students write about the things that interest them without the teacher's guidance. Some examples are diaries, invitations, e-mails, and personal notes to name a few.
- Procedure (based on Brown (2001) and Slattery & Willis (2001):
  (1) Give them time to think about what they are interested in.
  (2) Encourage them to choose a topic to write about.
  (3) Ask them to write about the chosen topic without stopping.
  (4) Spelling and grammar are not critical. The point is that they keep writing about the things that come to their minds.

5. Tasks for teaching writing

What is happening in the primary English writing classroom? We are going to have a close look at the writing tasks focused on alphabet letters, words or phrases, simple sentences, and simple texts.

1) Writing alphabet letters

The writing system of the Korean language is a lot different from that of the English language. Therefore, systematic instruction is needed for the children to know the English alphabet.

Brewster et al. (1991, p. 77) describe the following technique which students can try to learn new letters.

- Notice a letter shape and make a mental picture.

- Say the letter out loud and write it in the air with one finger.
- Write the letter on paper.
- See if the shape is correct.

Instead of forcing the children to copy the shapes at first sight, we had better follow the order of 'notice and then copy.'

In the following, our attention will be given to the examples of the alphabet writing tasks in the primary classrooms.

(1) Copying the English alphabet letters using pictures

When you teach the spelling of a new letter to children, first present a picture of a word which starts with the letter. Make sure that the new letters are connected to the sounds of the orally produced words.

- Write the letter on the dotted line.

- Write the letter without the dotted line.

(2) Writing the pairs of the capital/small letters

- Ex 1) ( ) a, B ( ), . . .
- Ex 2) Write the capital letters on the left to the small letters on the right.

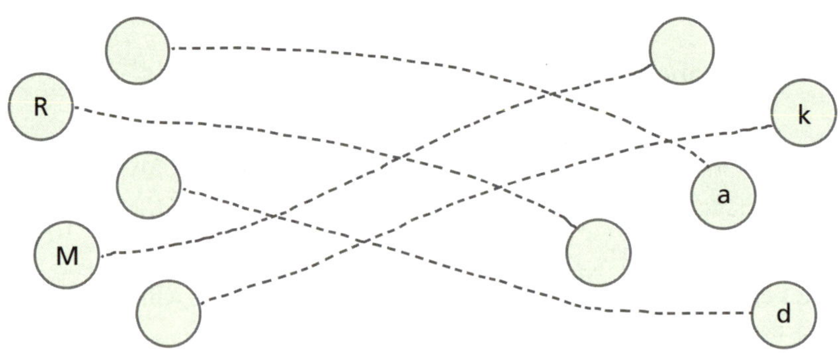

- Ex 3) Find the way through the maze and write the capital letters to the small ones.

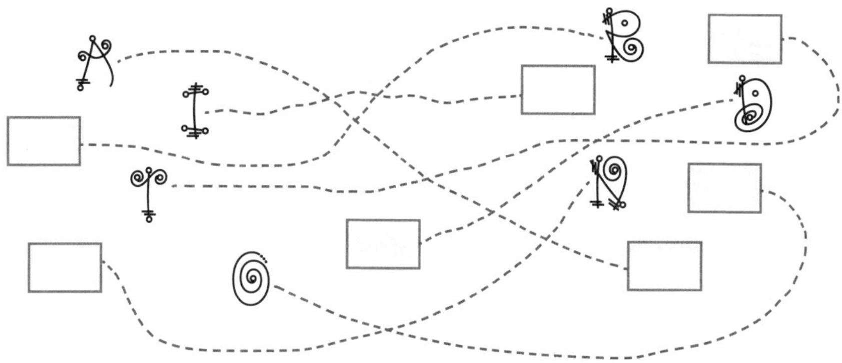

(3) Writing the letters in the order of *A(a)* to *Z(z)*

Besides the individual letters, we can also teach children the order of the English alphabet like in these examples:

- Write the alphabet letters in the blanks of the railway passenger cars.

- Write the alphabet letters in the blanks of the bricks.

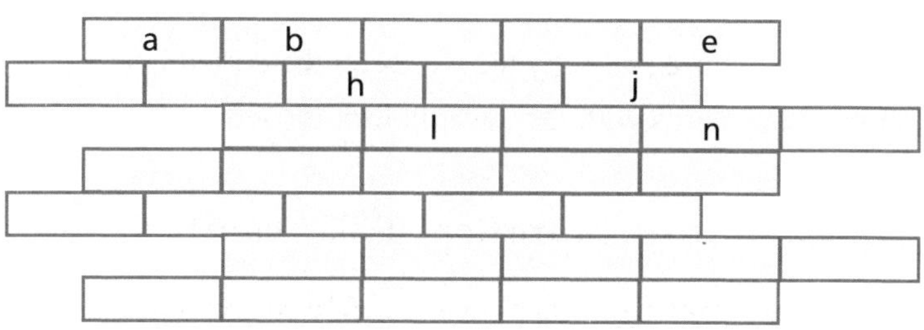

- G - □ - I - □ - K - □
- A b C ◯ E f ◯ h I j ◯ l

(4) Dictation of the alphabet letters

- Write the letters after listening to them.

(5) Alphabet writing games

① Alphabet letter making

· Make the alphabet letters out of play dough, baduk stones, cardboard and paper.

② Making the letters using a group of students' bodies

2) Writing words and phrases

To children in Korean classrooms, the main activity is writing words and phrases. Writing words and phrases is very important because it is the building blocks of the following levels.

(1) Copying

We can observe a lot of copying words and phrases in the classroom. The first step of writing is copying, but the point is how teachers encourage students to copy words without feeling bored. We teachers should think of more interesting ways of copying like these.

① Copying the words on the dotted line

- Look at the picture and copy the words on the dotted line.
- Complete the words with the lower half of the letters and copy them.

Spring Summer Fall Winter

Monday Tuesday Wednesday

March June October December

- Fill in the blanks to make them the same words.

  Ex) □olf - w□□□

  □able - t□□□□

② Copying the words after changing some letters

- Change the capital/small words to the small/capital words.
- Fill in the blanks with the suitable small letters using the picture and the capital letter of 'E' and 'I.'

  Ex) p□nc□l - E, I

③ Games for word copying

- Go down the ladder and copy the word at the bottom.
- Copy the words in the mirror.
- Find the suitable letters and complete the word.

  Ex) Some letters are written on the fish. Find the correct fish and fill in the blanks.

  a, g, h, i, e → E n _ l _ s h

- Find the words in the bag.

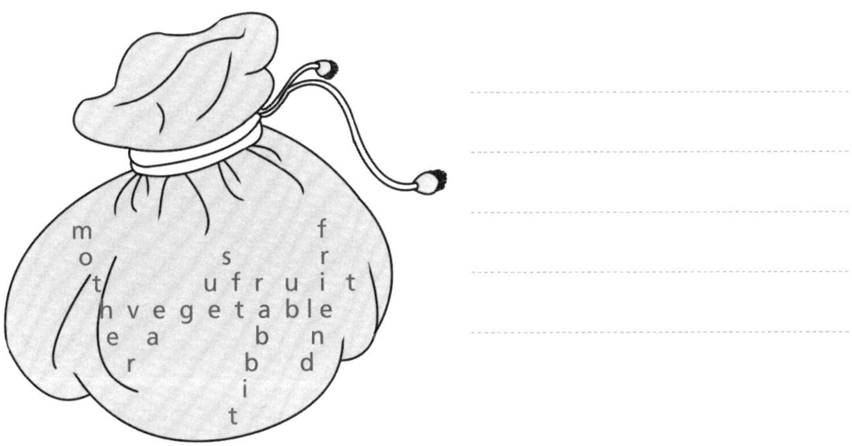

(2) Writing words appropriate to the pictures

① Matching the words to the pictures and writing them

- Find the correct words and write them under the appropriate pictures on the dotted line.
- Match and complete the partially written words to the pictures and write the words.

MAP BIRD ICE CREAM DESK

LION ROSE BANANA COMPUTER

② Completing the words using the pictures

Ex 1) 5 '_ i v e'

Ex 2) a□□□□ 

Ex 3) □ky 

③ Writing words using the pictures and the words in the example

- Find the correct words for clothes and write the names beside the suitable clothes.
- Find the correct words for the animals and write them beside their appropriate house.

④ Writing words next to the pictures

- Write the correct word beside each picture.

(3) Making words

① Completing words

a) Filling in the blanks with appropriate letters

- Choose the correct letter and fill in the blank.

Ex) □acket (i, j)

- Complete the words using the picture and the letters.

Ex)  + (o, p, t, s)

b□□ □□□□

b) Completing the two parts into one

Ex) Match the locks to the right keys.

② Writing words after unscrambling the letters

- Put the letters in order and write the right words.

Ex. 1)

① ________ yapph

② ________ das

③ ________ anrgy

Ex. 2) K O B O B□□□

③ Writing new words

- Make new words using the letters of the given words.

Ex) grandmother

⇒ he, to, hot, her, dog, net, red, get, tan, and, moth, mother, grand,

(4) Dictation of words

- Listen carefully and fill in the blanks with appropriate letters.
- Listen carefully and write the appropriate words for the pictures.
- Listen carefully and write the appropriate words in the 'example'.

(5) Completing the word puzzles

- Complete the words using the pictures and write a new word using the □ in the order of the above pictures.

Ex) □ki - □iano - t□nt - □pple - s□ate

→□□□□□

- Unscramble the letters on the left, and write them on the right. And then write a new word using the ▣ in the order of their numbers.

(1) g, n, e, d, r, a	▣ □ □ □ □ □
(2) n, i, r, a	▣ □ □ □
(3) e, c, a, k	□ □ □ ▣
(4) a, e, h, r	□ □ ▣ □
(5) e, t, e, m	□ □ □ ▣
	□ □ □ □ □

(6) Word search and write

- Write the words using the pictures and find them in the word search.
- Write the words after listening to them and find them in the word search.

(7) Activity for word writing

- Make a picture dictionary.

apple ball cat . . .

3) Writing sentences

(1) Copying the sentences

- Read the sentences with pictures and copy them on the dotted line.
- Copy the sentences paying attention to the punctuation.
- Find the same sentences and copy them.

(2) Rewriting sentences

① Connecting the sentences to the correct pictures and then rewriting the sentences.

- Rewrite the sentence like the example.

Ex.) I can eat · · 

→ I can eat with my mouth.

I can hear · · 

→ I can hear with ( ).

② Rewriting the sentence by changing the subject like the example

Ex) I go to school by bike → He goes to school by bike.

I walk to school every day. → ______________________.

③ Changing two sentences into one sentence

- Connect two sentences into one sentence using the correct connecting words.

Chris likes tennis.	and	I go on holiday in the summer.
I work in the winter.	but	I like my job.
Kim lives in New York.	so	He doesn't like volleyball.
I work in an office.	because	He likes big cities.

(3) Correcting the errors

① The capital / small letters

- Correct the errors and write the correct sentence in the blank.

  Ex) how's Ellen doing? → ______________________________.

② Spacing

- Mark the places to space and write the correct sentence.

  Ex) Howdoyoulikeit? → ______________________________.

③ Capital / small letter, spacing and punctuation

- Write the sentences again using appropriate capital/small letter, punctuation and spacing.

  Ex 1) what did the doctor say. → ______________________________.

  Ex 2) CANISPEAKTOALICE → ____________________.

  Ex 3) go Straight AND turn Left → ________________________.

(4) Writing sentences after arranging the scrambled words

① Write sentences after arranging the scrambled letters.

- Ex 1) I want to be an <u>ngseri</u>. → ______________________________.
- Ex 2)

h, o, w, e, s	o, p, e, t, u, c, m, r	s, i	h, i, t, s	?

____

② Write sentences after unscrambling words.

- Ex 1) coming / vacation / summer

  → The______ ______ is ______ soon.

- Ex 2) Arrange the scrambled words using the picture.

Su-nam   tennis   often   on Saturday   plays

(5) Completing the sentences using the pictures

- Ex 1)
  There are some  ______________________.

- Ex 2)
  'Can you ______ me?' 

- Ex 3) It takes an hour by  ______.

- Ex 4)
  · ○ ○ ○ → Draw ______________
  · □□ → Draw ______________

(6) Completing the short dialogue

① Arrange the words to complete the dialogue.
Ex) A: ______________ this Sunday?
(to, what, going, you, are, do)
B: ________ the zoo.
(to, going, I'm)

② Complete the dialogue by unscrambling the words.

Ex 1) A: Do you like tennis?

B: Yes. ________________________________.

(me, father, tennis, my, teaches)

Ex 2) Write a short dialogue using the words.

is calling
Who's please
Su-jin This

A: ____________________, ______________?

B: ____________________________________.

③ Complete the dialogue using proper words for the situation.

I am from Korea.

____________________?

____

Canada.

(7) Writing sentences after listening to them

- Ex 1) Listen to the sentence carefully and arrange the words.
  · did what yesterday you do → ________________________________.

- Ex 2) Listen to the dialogue carefully and arrange the words using the pictures.

A: __________________________________?

(did, yesterday, what, do, you)

B: __________________________________.

(did my I homework)

- Ex 3) Listen to the sentences carefully and fill in the blanks using the words in the example.

Example: comb wash brush

1) I'm _________ my face.
2) Mijin _________ her hair every morning.
3) Sunam _________ his teeth after lunch.

(8) Writing sentences using puzzles

- Ex 1)

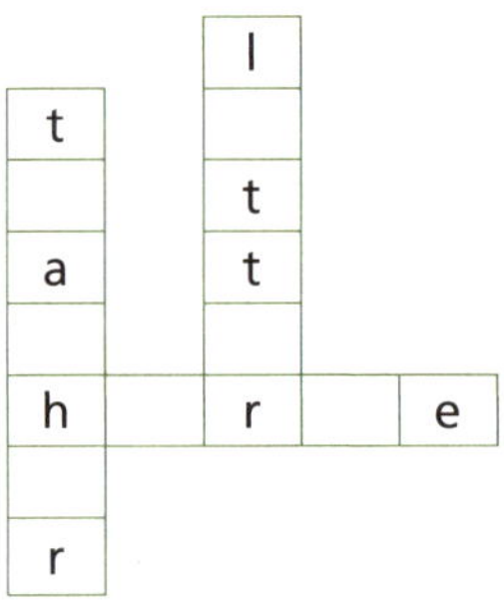

1) The (   ) imitates the (   ).

2) She is writing a (   ) to her friend.

- Ex 2) Write a sentence using the first letters of each picture in the order of ① to ⑨.

① 토요일

② 

③ 

④ 

⑤ 

⑥ 

⑦ 

⑧ 

⑨ 

□□□ □□ □□□□

(9) Translating Korean into English

- Ex 1) you ? for sing Will us
  우리를 위하여 노래를 해 주겠니? → ____________________________.

- Ex 2) 만나서 반갑습니다. → Nice to ______________.

- Ex 3) 얼마나 자주 운동하니? → How _____ do you _______?

- Ex 4) 그건 너무 짧아요. → It's t _____ sh _____.

- Ex 5) 미안합니다. → ______________.

4) Writing simple texts

(1) Writing a simple story

① Copying the model sentences

- Follow the faded verbs and copy the sentences.

Every day he wakes up at 7 in the morning.
He stretches his arms and rubs his eyes and he **yawns**.
Then he brushes his teeth.
He puts on his clothes and eats his breakfast.
At 8 he leaves his house.
He walks to school.

② Writing new sentences by changing some parts of the model

- Write your dreams changing the underlined words.

Our Dreams

We have dreams. I want to be <u>a teacher</u>. My friend, <u>Mi-jin</u>, wants to be <u>a doctor</u>. We hope to be a good <u>teacher</u> and a good <u>doctor</u>.

- Su-nam visited his cousins last Sunday. Write about his visit to his cousins by changing the bold words.

Visit to Cousins

Su-nam **wants** to visit his cousins.
They live in the country. He **takes** the train.
He **goes fishing** in the lake, and he **rides a bike** in the park.
He **is** very tired, but he **is** very happy.

→ Su-nam __________ to visit his cousins.
They __________ in the country. He __________ the train.
He __________ in the lake, and he __________ in the park.
He __________ very tired, but he __________ very happy.

③ Arranging and organizing

- Arrange the sentences and make two stories.
  (a) The child who was sitting behind the bear couldn't see.
  (b) "That's why the coffee's not very good." the bear said.
  (c) "He likes baseball." the woman said. "Now he wants to watch a game."

(d) A woman once took her bear friend to the baseball stadium.
(e) The waiter gave one to him and the bear drank it.
(f) One day a bear went into a cafe and asked for a cup of honey tea.
(g) "Why did you bring this bear here?" he asked.
(h) "We don't see many bears in here," the waiter said.

④ Writing a text using model sentences
- Write your everyday routine using the model.
- Write about your dad or mom using the model.
- Write about Sports Day using the model pictures.

(2) Keeping a diary

① Copying the model diary
- Recognize the components of a diary.
- Correct the errors and copy the sentences.

> Sunday, november 11, Fine
> Today is my birthday. I have a wonderful party
> with my family?
> I have a good time

- Arrange and organize the sentences, and copy the sentences.

② Keeping your diary by changing the model diary
- Keep your diary using the model diary with scrambled sentences.
- Keep your diary using the model diary with the daily routine phrases.
- Keep your diary using the model pictures.

I went to school at 8. ______________________________

____

____

____

③ Keeping your own diary

- Write about last weekend.
- Write about a special event.

(3) Writing an invitation card

- Copy the model invitation card.
- Complete the model invitation after listening to it.

Ellen

Please j□□□ us

for □□□□□□mas party.

Jimin and Jisun

- Write your invitation to your birthday party using the model form.

To ______________________

Please come to my birthday party

on ______________________

From ______________ till ______________

At ______________________________

From ____________________

(4) Writing a letter

Letters include a short note, a text message, e-mail etc. Tasks for writing a letter should be presented step by step considering the students' abilities.

- Copy the model letter after changing the underlined words.
- Complete the letter with the blanks using the words in the example.
- Complete the letter with the blanks and then write a new letter.
- Write a new letter using the model letter.

Ex) Write a letter to Santa Claus about yourself.

Dear Santa,

My name is ______________________.

I am a student ______________________.

I am ______________________ old.

I have been a good ______________________ this year.

I really want ______________________.

I hope you can give this to me.

Best wishes,

Tom Brown

6. Practice of teaching writing in the primary classroom

How do primary English teachers teach writing in their classrooms? We will see an example below. Ms. Kim teaches 'Let's Write' of 'Lesson 7. My father is a pilot (MEST, 2009, pp. 60~61 (Elementary school English 6))' to sixth graders.

(1) 다음 문장을 써 봅시다.

My father is a cook.

My mother is a teacher.

My uncle is a pilot.

(2) 그림을 보고 문장을 써 봅시다.

My grandfather is a cook.

My father is a pilot.

My brother is a teacher.

My sister is a police.

Before-writing

T	It's time to write! Look at your book on page 60.
Ss	(Open their books)
T	Let's look at the first one. Who do you see in this picture?
Ss	요리사요! Cook!
T	Great! There's a cook. How about the second one?
Ss	Teacher!
T	Right. Teacher! There's a teacher like me! Third picture?
Ss	Pilot!
T	Good! There's a pilot. Can you read the sentences under the pictures?
Ss	(Ss try to read them aloud.)
T	Repeat after me! (My father is a cook.) (My mother is a teacher.) (I want to be a pilot.) Good job! This time let's watch the TV. Please, watch carefully how to write it. (A teacher shows how to write the sentences with the CD-ROM)
T	Well done. Let's write the sentences with your finger in the air.
Ss	(Ss write the sentences with their fingers in the air.)
T	Good. Let's write the sentences in your book. Please, try to write them in order.
Ss	Yes!

While-writing

Ss	(Each student writes the sentences in their book.)
T	Are you done?
Ss	Yes!
T	Well done! Shall we move to the next? This is a pair activity. One writes a sentence on the back of your classmate. The other writes the sentence on the sheet. The team which writes the sentences correctly will be the winner. Is it clear? (A teacher shows an example.)
Ss	Yes. (Do the activity)
T	Great! Let's move on to a second activity. Open your books to page 61.
Ss	(Open their books)
T	Do you see the small pictures?
Ss	Yes, I do.
T	There are some clues for the sentence in the pictures. Look at the first picture. Who do you see in the first picture?
Ss	Grandfather! Doctor!
T	Good! Can you make a sentence with "Grandfather" and "Doctor"? Try it, please.
S1	Grandfather is doctor!
T	Nice try! Good! Is there anyone who can make it a little better? For example, my grandfather...
S2	My grandfather is doctor!
T	Great! Getting better! Anyone else?
S3	My grandfather is a doctor!
T	Well done! You guys made a perfect sentence! You can make a sentence with the clues in the pictures in this way. Can you do it?

Ss	Yes!
T	OK. Do it by yourself first and then try to do it with your group.

Post-writing

T	Are you done? Here's a sheet. I'll give your group this sheet. Write all the sentences you created in your group. (A teacher gives Ss a big paper)
Ss	(Do the activity)
T	Have you done it?
Ss	Yeah!
T	OK. Let's check it. Which group goes first?
Ss	Me! Me! Here!
T	OK. You go first!
Ss	(Have Ss present what they have done.)
T	Excellent! Beautiful! You all did a great job. Let's write the sentences with your finger in the air reading aloud.

Questions for discussion

(1) In the pre-writing activities, how does the teacher encourage students to write each sentence? Do you think those techniques are useful in the writing classroom?

(2) In the while-writing activities, what does the teacher do before students write each sentence?

(3) In the post-writing activities, students write all the sentences they created in their group. Do you think this task is meaningful to the children? If yes, why?

Part II

Teaching activities using the four language skills

5. Teaching Songs

6. Teaching Games

7. Teaching Stories

8. Teaching Role play

5 Teaching Songs

In this chapter, we will look at the following questions regarding teaching songs in primary English classrooms:

1) What is the purpose of using songs in the classroom?
2) What are the types of children's songs?
3) How can we teach the songs and are there other activities we can use?
4) How can songs be adapted to specific needs?
5) Is there any model procedure for teaching songs in the classroom?

1. Why use songs?

Why do lots of teachers teach songs in the classroom? That is because they know how much children enjoy songs and how easy it is to memorize words, phrases and sentences. These activities provide a link with home and school life and are often lively and fun as shown in Brewster (1991), Cross (1995), and Paul (2003).

(1) Variety

- Variety is added to the range of learning situations.
- Songs can add feeling and rhythm to somewhat flat language practice, thus helping children remember things easily.

(2) Confidence

- Children's participation is encouraged, and in a group activity giving confidence to shy children.
- Children show off their songs to the family and give them confidence in language learning.

(3) Motivation

- The pace of a lesson can be changed, thus maintaining students' motivation.

(4) Language practice

- Hidden practice of specific language patterns and vocabulary can be provided.
- Children-children communication is increased, which provides fluency practice and reduces the domination of the class by the teacher.
- Listening skills, attention span and concentration are improved.

(5) The prosodic features of English

- Children can be accustomed automatically to the prosodic features of the English language such as stress, rhythm, intonation and syllable length, etc.

(6) Cultural understanding

- Songs and rhymes also give insight into the target culture. They are authentic texts.

2. Types of songs

There are many children's songs for the primary classrooms. In the following we will have a close look at the two types of children's songs, 'Action songs,' and 'Traditional songs.'

1) Action songs

Children can mime the actions as they sing. This makes children physically and emotionally immersed in the class. Doing the actions helps them memorize the meaning of the words. Therefore, these kinds of action songs can be used especially for the younger children.

Example 1

Teddy bear, teddy bear, touch the ground, [touch floor]
Teddy bear, teddy bear, turn around, [turn]
Teddy bear, teddy bear, walk upstairs, [climb stairs]
Teddy bear, teddy bear, say your prayers, [put palms together]
Teddy bear, teddy bear, turn out the light, [turn out light]
Teddy bear, teddy bear, say goodnight. [jump out of the rope] [wave goodbye]

(based on Brewster, 1991, p. 175)

Example 2

1. The wheels on the bus go round and round, round and round, round and round, the wheels on the bus go round and round, all through the town.
2. The people on the bus go up and down, up and down, up and down.
3. The horn on the bus goes beep, beep, beep, beep, beep, beep, beep, beep, beep.
4. The wipers on the bus go swish swish swish, swish, swish, swish, swish, swish, swish.
5. The signals on the bus go blink, blink, blink, blink, blink, blink, blink, blink, blink.
6. The motor on the bus goes zoom, zoom, zoom, zoom, zoom, zoom, zoom, zoom, zoom.
7. The babies on the bus go waa, waa, waa, waa, waa, waa, waa, waa, waa
8. The parents on the bus go shh, shh, shh, shh, shh, shh, shh, shh, shh.

(http://bussongs.com/songs)

Example 3: I'm a little teapot

I'm a little teapot, short and stout.
(short - shrink a bit, stout - expand arms sideways)
Here is my handle, here is my spout,
(handle - put a hand on one hip, spout - curve other arm in the shape of a spout)
When I get all steamed up, then I shout.
(swirl hands upwards then make hands a megaphone for the mouth)
Just tip me over, and pour me out.
(lean over to the spout side) (based on Paul, 2003, pp. 59~60)

2) Traditional songs

Example 1: Old Macdonald had a farm

Old Macdonald had a farm, ee aye ee aye oh.
And on that farm he had some chickens, ee aye ee aye oh.
Chorus:
With a cluck cluck here, a cluck cluck there,
Here a cluck, there a cluck, everywhere a cluck cluck,
Old Macdonald had a farm, ee aye ee aye oh.

Old Macdonald had a farm, ee aye ee aye oh.
And on that farm he had some dogs, ee aye ee aye oh.
Chorus:
With a woof woof here, a woof woof there,
Here a woof, there a woof, everywhere a woof woof,
Old Macdonald had a farm, ee aye ee aye oh. (http://www.kididdles.com/lyrics)

Children can extend the song by adding both animals and their sounds such as ducks *(quack quack*), sheep (*baa baa*), cows (*moo moo*), cats (*miaow miaow*), turkeys (*gobble gobble*), pigs (*oink oink*) etc.

Example 2: Here we go round the mulberry bush.

Here we go round the mulberry bush,
The mulberry bush, the mulberry bush,
Here we go round the mulberry bush,
So early in the morning.

(The following is an alternate version based on 'Here we go round the mulberry bush.')
This is the way we wash our clothes,
Wash our clothes, wash our clothes,
This is the way we wash our clothes,
So early Monday morning.

This is the way we iron our clothes,
Iron our clothes, iron our clothes,
This is the way we iron our clothes,
So early Tuesday morning.

This is the way we scrub the floor,
Scrub the floor, scrub the floor,
This is the way we scrub the floor,
So early Wednesday morning. (http://bussongs.com/songs)

Any daily routine can be added: *brush our teeth, wash our face, comb our hair, sweep the floor, bake our bread, wash the dishes, mend our clothes etc.*

Example 3: Row, row, row your boat

This song was originally sung by slaves rowing on the Mississippi though it is one of the most popular children's songs. The words are only meaningful in this sense. This song is short but sounds very sweet, so children can sing this as a four part round. If you want to extend this song, go to the website (http://www.songsforteaching.com).

Row, row, row your boat,
gently down the stream
Merrily, merrily, merrily, merrily,
life is but a dream.

Example 4: Twinkle, Twinkle, Little Star

Twinkle, twinkle, little star,
How I wonder what you are,
Up above the world so high,
Like a diamond in the sky,
Twinkle, twinkle, little star,
How I wonder what you are. (http://www.kididdles.com)

3. Ways of teaching songs in the classroom

How can we teach children to sing? When teachers can sing well, they sing the song, and then children repeat it. When they do not sing well, they turn on the CD-ROM, and then children repeat the song. We will have a look at more details for teaching songs in the classroom based on Brewster (1991), Cross (1995), and Paul (2003).

1) Before singing activities

- Focus questions: Put some focus questions on the blackboard or worksheet to guide the class in listening to the song.
- Private study: This is another good way to approach a longer piece. After a fairly rapid and silent reading, the students ask for any needed explanations. This may be done in English or the mother tongue, depending on the level of the class. Many children's English songs are already translated into Korean, so it may surprise the children who will know the music and must only learn the English words.

2) Presentation of the song

- You illustrate the song line by line with pictures and you demonstrate the actions.
- You can translate the song into the Korean language.

3) Singing activities

- Learning singing: Listen and repeat the song line by line after the teacher or the CD-ROM.
- Individualized singing: The songs can be sung by the whole class, or you may like to vary the groupings such as half the class, large groups, small groups, pairs or individuals, etc.
- Cloze texts: Write the text on the board, poster or hand-out, but with key words or phrases deleted. The student pairs have to identify the missing words as they listen.
- Disappearing texts: You put the whole text on the blackboard. The students read it as they listen. Afterwards they sing or recite it. Then, one or two words are erased and it is sung again. More words are erased, and so on until it can be sung with no support. This is an enjoyable and challenging way to get shorter texts learned by heart.

4) After singing activities

- Drawing: Children can simply draw a picture that illustrates the song and write some words related to the song.
- Dictation: Teachers can ask children to dictate the words or sentences in the song.
- Puzzles: Children do puzzles such as crosswords or word searches with the words from the song.

4. Examples of teaching some songs

Example 1: Ten little Indian boys (COUNTING SONG)

a) Presentation: Tell the class they will hear a song about Indians. Show a picture of a native North American Indian and mention cowboy films.
b) Visual cue: Write the numbers 1 to 10 on the blackboard, with the picture of the Indian in the middle.
c) Look and listen: Play or sing the song two or three times, pointing to the numbers as they occur in the song.
d) Repetition: Have the class repeat line by line, paying great attention to the rhythmic pattern which represents the sounds of Indian drums, with one stressed syllable (italicized parts) followed by two unstressed ones.
e) Singing: Get the class singing, ensuring that only the correct syllables are stressed;

One little, *two* little, *three* little *In*dians,
Four little, *five* little, *six* little *In*dians,
Seven little *eight* little, *nine* little *In*dians,
Ten little *In*dian *boys.*
(There were:)
Ten little, *nine* little, *eight* little *In*dians,

Seven little, *six* little, *five* little *In*dians,
four little, *three* little, *two* little *In*dians,
One little *In*dian *boy*!

(based on Cross, 1995, 167-171)

Example 2: If you're happy and you know it

a) Presentation:

- Translation: The structure 'If you're happy and you know it' is a little difficult for some children, so it can be translated into Korean.
- Demonstration: Teachers can do the actions to the emotion 'Happy' and the imperative 'Clap your hands.'

b) Singing: With the cue visible on the blackboard, children are standing up or moving around. The class can sing in chorus. Later, individuals can sing, while the other students mime the actions.

1. If you're happy and you know it, clap your hands, [clap hands twice]
   If you're happy and you know it, clap your hands, [clap hands twice]
   If you're happy and you know it, and you really want to show it,
   If you're happy and you know it, clap your hands, [clap hands twice]

(based on http://www.kididdles.com/lyrics)

c) Singing again

Teachers can invent new actions to the emotion 'Happy.' And then children can extend the original song by adding 'Nod your heads,' 'Touch your nose,' 'Tap your toes,' etc. respectively.

2. If you're happy and you know it, tap your toes, [tap toes twice]
3. If you're happy and you know it, nod your heads, [nod head]
4. If you're happy and you know it, turn around, [turn around]

d) Adapting the song: teachers can adapt the song either by changing some parts or by making the original song simpler like the examples in Paul (2003, pp. 65~66).

(1) Adapt the song by changing some parts.

Teacher can change 'Happy' to different emotions like 'angry' or 'tired.' And imperatives can be changed to 'Stamp your feet,' or 'Go to bed.'

(2) Making the song simpler

The structure 'If you're happy and you know it' may be too difficult for some children. Therefore, it can be simpler like this.

Are you happy? Are you happy?
Are you happy? Are you happy? Clap your hands.
Are you happy? Are you happy? Clap your hands.
Are you happy? Are you happy? Yes, we are very happy.
Are you happy? Are you happy? Clap your hands.

5. Practice of teaching songs in the primary classroom

How do primary English teachers teach songs in their classrooms? We will see an example in the following. Ms. Kim teaches 'Let's Sing' of 'Lesson 7. My father is a pilot (MEST, 2009, p. 60 (Elementary school English 6))' to sixth graders.

▶ Title of the song: People in my town

I see a pilot flying through the air.
I see a firefighter fighting fires.
I see the barber cutting people's hair.
I see a car mechanic changing tires.

I see the people in my town and I say,
Hey, brother, what's going down?

I see a lifeguard at the swimming pool.
I see the postman with the mail.
I see the teacher in the local schools.
I see the police putting folk in jail.

I see the people in my town and I say,
Hey, brother, what's going down?
Doctors, nurses, astronauts, judges, lawyers in the courts.

I see a chef working in a restaurant
and a waiter asking what you want.
I see an actor acting on the stage.
I see a writer writing on a page.

I see the people in my town and I say,
Hey, brother, what's going down?
Doctors, nurses, astronauts, judges, lawyers in the courts.

(http://www.youtube.com/watch?v=JBXaupIJHr8)

Before listening to the song

T	It's time for a song!
Ss	Ye~!
T	Can you guess what we are going to sing?
Ss	노래요.. 60쪽 노래요.. (시시하다는 듯이)
T	Nice try! But.. no!!
Ss	교과서 60쪽 노래요!
T	I said no! (showing the freeze-frame of the video clip) We are going to sing a different song from the textbook. Can you guess what the song is about?
Ss	(watching the freeze-frame) Um.. 직업요, 직업!
T	Great! Please, say it in English. How can you say 직업 in English?
Ss	Job요!
T	Good! We've learned about many jobs, such as a doctor, driver, nurse, pilot, police, singer and so on. Jobs, right?
Ss	Yes!
T	Is there anyone who knows the title of the song? Can you guess?
S2	(trying to read the freeze-frame) People.. in my.. town?
T	Wonderful! As S2 said, the title of the song is "People in my town". Repeat after me, people in my town! (read slowly)
Ss	People in my town!
T	People in my town! (with a normal speed)
S2	People in my town!
T	Good! Now let's listen to the song, first. (have the students listen to the song with the video clip) Here we go~! (Watch the video clip)

Post-listening

T	Did you listen well? Tell me how many jobs you heard.
Ss	Doctor! Nurse! Pilot! Teacher! Postman! Police! Actor!
T	(Students and a teacher count the jobs together) OK. 7 jobs? Anything else?
S3	Writer?
T	Great! Writer! 8 jobs! Anything else? (mime to chop something on the chopping board) Can you guess?
Ss	아.. 아.. 요리사!
S4	Che..Chef!
T	Good job! Anything else?
S6	한번 더 봐요! 한번 더요!
T	Do you want to watch it one more time?
S6	Yes! Yes! One more time! One more time!
T	Okay. Try to figure out which jobs there are. Here we go~!

After listening to the song

T	How was it? Did you enjoy it?
Ss	Yes! 재미있어요.
T	Pop quiz! How many jobs are there in this song?
Ss	(웅성거린다)
T	Is there anyone who knows how many jobs are in this song?
Ss	10개요! 20개요!
T	OK. Let's watch it again and figure it out.
Ss	Yes!
T	Everybody, are you ready?
Ss	Yeah~!
T	OK. Here we go. (have the students listen to the song again with the video clip)

Questions for discussion

(1) The teacher does not use the song in the textbook. What do you think about her decision?

(2) What are the steps that the teacher uses to teach the song? Can you think of any other steps to use?

(3) Grade Six students rarely enjoy singing in class. What other music based activities can you bring into the classroom? What other source of music can you use other than the textbook?

6 Teaching Games

In regards to teaching games in primary English classrooms, we will look into the following questions:

1) What is the definition of games?
2) How are games beneficial in the primary classroom?
3) What types of games are appropriate for the primary classroom?
4) What should teachers consider when using games?
5) How should games be taught?
6) Is there any model procedure for teaching games in the primary classroom?

1. What are games?

What are games or play? Do they mean the same thing or are they different? What do games or play really mean? Let's look them up in the dictionary.

- First, according to the Dictionary of English Education (Jo & Lee, 2004, p. 307), games are physical or mental activities for achieving the preset objectives through cooperation or competition following rules, and they are pleasant and challenging. But, with play the element of competition is not fully emphasized, so it is different from games.

- Second, Longman Dictionary of Applied Linguistics (Richards, Platt & Weber, 1985, p. 118) defines games as 'an organized activity that usually has the following properties: (a) a particular task or objective, (b) a set of rules, (c) a competition between players, (d) communication between players by spoken or written language .'

2. What are the benefits of games?

They say that children enjoy games. Teachers often remember that children have asked you to play games. Why do teachers really use games in the classrooms?

1) Motivation

- Motivation is enhanced by play and competition.
- Language learning is hard work. Games help and encourage many learners to sustain their interest.

2) Acquisition

- The learners' attention is on the message, not on the language. Therefore, they acquire language unconsciously, with their whole attention engaged by the activity, in the same way they acquired their first language.

3) Meaningful contexts for learning

- Games help the teacher to create contexts in which the language is useful and meaningful. The learners want to take part and in order to do so must understand what others are saying or have written, and they must speak or write in order to express their own point of view or give information (Wright, Betteridge, & Buckby, 1983, pp. 1~2).
- Games provide a nonthreatening environment for coping with new learning. When children are having fun, they are more likely to take risks, and make mistakes without having feelings of failure (Paul, 2003, p. 49).

- Through games, learners practice and internalize vocabulary, grammar and structures.

4) Flexibility of lessons

- Games are easily fitted into any lesson plan. This gives teachers lots of flexibility. So lessons become less predictable. Variety enhances the motivation in the classroom activity.

3. Kinds of games

- What kinds of games are there in language learning? There are picture games, card games, board games, question and answer games, guessing games, word games, memory games, information gap games, problem solving games, etc.
- Games can be divided into 'language practice games' or 'communication games,' based on the purpose of playing the games (Brewstar, 1991, pp. 180~181). The former aim to practice new language items and develop accuracy, often taking the form of hidden drills. The purpose is usually to score more points than others and there is often a clear winner. In communication games, the children are expected to draw upon any of their linguistic resources to complete the task. Therefore, language practice games are more likely to be played with the whole class or teams, while communication games are often played in pairs or small groups .
- Games also can be sorted according to language skills such as listening games, speaking games, reading games, and writing games (See 'Appendix' at the end of this chapter).

4. Things to consider when teachers use games in the classrooms

1) Variety in the choice of the games

Bear in mind that different from language games, communication games focus on co-operation and are more likely to give every child a chance to have a turn to speak in an unthreatening atmosphere.

2) Forming groups with the help of the group leaders

Each group leader will be responsible for collecting equipment, giving it out, explaining details to the group and putting equipment away. Make sure that the role of group leader is given to different students so that they can all take a turn.

3) Giving clear instructions

The teacher must ensure that very clear instructions are given before and during the game. You will probably do this in the mother tongue. Always try to give a demonstration, using any necessary resources and one or two of the children .

4) Active participation in the game

Teachers need to step in to ensure the games are challenging the children to extend their ability while they are playing (Brewstar, 1991, pp. 182~184; Paul, 2003, pp. 52~55).

- We can add more difficult, but achievable, words and patterns as they play.
- We can talk with them while they are playing, using language that is natural and understandable from the context such as, 'It's my turn!' and 'Go ahead three squares'.
- We can help by scaffolding their language as they play games. We sometimes use patterns that are just beyond the ones that the children are able to use by themselves, encouraging them to move beyond what they know now.
- We can make funny sounds, often using a puppet or class mascot, when the children make mistakes we think they should reflect on.

5. How to teach games

- How do teachers introduce games to students and teach them to play games? It is often observed in classrooms that students are engaged in playing games, but they do not know what to say and how to play. Before the game, students should be well-informed on what to say and how to play.

- In the following, we will see a more detailed look at how to teach games in the primary classrooms based on Wright, Betteridge, & Buckby (1983, p. 6).

1) Noticing

- Teachers give students opportunities to think about the game. During a short break, students may be able to determine what to say and how to play.

2) Explanation of the rules of the game

- Teachers explain the rules of the game in a simple and clear way.
- Teachers can use the mother tongue depending on the students' language abilities.

3) Demonstration of the game:

- Teachers demonstrate the game using some of the students as models.

4) Playing the game in groups

- Form groups such as pairs, small groups, large groups, half class, whole class, etc. variously.

5) Teachers monitor the group activities

- Teachers answer students' questions.
- Teachers note down students' errors. Except for critical errors, avoid immediate correction so as not to interrupt the natural flow of the games.

6) Evaluation

- Students reflect on the following questions like 'Is the game interesting?' 'Is the difficulty level of the game appropriate to each student?' 'Do you like to play such games later?' etc.
- The teacher isolates the target language items on the board.

6. Practice of teaching games in the primary classroom

How do primary English teachers teach games in their classrooms? We will see an example in the following. Mr. Kim teaches 'Let's Play' of 'Lesson 3. How old are you? (MEST, 2009, p. 30 (Elementary school English 4))' to fourth graders.

Pre-activity

T	Now, we are going to play a game.
Ss	Wow! Dice game.
T	Do you like games with dice?
Ss	Of course.
T	Very good. First, can you count the numbers?

Ss	Yes, we can. (Counting numbers from one to six.)
T	Well done! Now, do you know how to play?
Ss	Um... Throw two dice and ...
T	You are right. Throw two dice and add what?
Ss	Numbers.
T	Right. Throw two dice and add two numbers. Everybody, can you do this?
Ss	Sure, we can.
T	Then, throw your dice and add the two numbers.
S1	(Throwing two dice) Five and six. It's eleven.
S2	It's six.
S3	Eight.
T	Wonderful! You did a good job! Who is the winner?
Ss	S1.
T	You are right. S1 has the largest number. Class, give a big hand to S1.
Ss	(Clapping their hands.)
T	Now, you are ready to start the game?
Ss	Sure, let's play.

While-activity

T	Now, let's play the 'Dice Game.'
Ss	Wow!
T	Very good! First, let's make groups of six, three boys and three girls. Boys are team A, and girls are team B
Ss	(Form groups of three boys and three girls)
T	Team A, raise your hands.
Ss	(Boys raise their hands.)
T	Good! This time, team B, raise your hands.
Ss	(Girls raise their hands.)
T	Very good! Now, I'll tell you how to play the game. Who will start first? Each group can decide. You can do rock-paper-scissors. Or, you can toss a coin.
Ss	(Each group decides each team's turn.)
T	First team, stand up.
Ss	(All the first teams stand up.)
T	Good! And, each team picks who will throw two dice first, second, and last.
Ss	(Each team picks who will throw two dice first, second, and last.)
T	Good! Now, the second team asks, 'How old are you?' And, one from the first team, throw two dice, and add the two numbers. Finally, the student answers the question. Do you understand?
Ss	Yes.
T	Now, the first team's turn ends. Next, one from the second team throws two dice. And, you play the game in the same way.

S1	Who wins the game?
T	Good question!
	After each round, find the difference between each pair of sums.
	The bigger sum gets the difference.
	After three rounds, the team with the larger number wins the game.
	Is this clear?
Ss	Yes.

Post-activity

T	Did you enjoy the game?
Ss	Sure.
T	Which team won the game?
	Winners, raise your hands.
Ss	(The winners raise their hands.)
T	Very good!
Ss	Can we play another game?
T	Why not?
Ss	Wow!
T	This time, let's change the rules.
	Each round, the smaller sum gets the difference.
	After three rounds, the team with the larger numbers wins the game.
	Do you understand?
Ss	Yes.
T	(After the game)
	How was the game?
Ss	Can we play the game again?
T	Sorry, not now. We will play the game again later.
Ss	I see.

T	Good! Before we go, let's review, 'How old are you?' and 'I'm --- years old.'
T	You ask me, 'How old are you?' And, I throw two dice and answer. Right?
Ss	Yes.
T	Ask, 'How old are you?'
Ss	How old are you?
T	(Throw two dice and add the numbers) I'm --- years old. Ask again.
T/Ss	(Students ask, 'How old are you?' And, teacher answers the questions.)
T	This time, I need a helper.
Ss	Me! Me! Me!
T/Ss	(Student volunteers throw two dice and play the game in this way.)

Questions for discussion

(1) What does the teacher do for the pre-activity? Do you think those introductions help students to play the game?

(2) Do you think the teacher's instruction for the game is appropriate to the students' linguistic levels?

(3) What is the post-activity for the game? Do you think it is a suitable activity for the game?

(4) Although games have been given a recommended age level, there are many ways to change the rules and subjects to make them more difficult or easier. Choose one game and change it to make it harder or easier.

Appendix: Examples of games

1. Listening games

1) Simon Says

- Aim: Understanding imperatives through body movement
- Level: 3rd grade
- Material: None
- Procedure:
    · The teacher presents the game with some students.
    · Students stand in a circle. If they do not follow the game, they are out. And so they go outside the circle. When the teacher says, 'Simon Says,' students do as the teacher says. But, when the teacher does not say, 'Simon Says,' students do not do as the teacher says.
    · Later, students can play again. This time, when the teacher says, 'Simon Says,' students do not move. And, when the teacher does not say, 'Simon Says,' students can move.
- Example:

T: Today we're going to play an interesting game. It's really interesting. Listen carefully. Shhh! Stop talking! Su-nam! Thank you. When I say 'Simon says', you should do what I say. And when I don't say 'Simon says', you must keep still. Don't move. If you move when I don't say 'Simon says', you're out. You have to go to the back of the classroom and wait for the next game. Are you ready to start? Now let's see who's listening.

T: Stand up. (No one moves.)

T: Simon says, 'Stand up.' (Everyone stands up.)

T: Very good. You're all listening.

T: Simon says, 'Turn around'. (Everyone turns around.)

T: 'Turn around.' (Some children turn around.)

T: Oh, oh! You did it and I didn't say 'Simon says'! OK, you go to the back of the classroom. OK.

T: Now, fly like a bird. (No one moves.) (based on Slattery & Willis, 2001, p. 30)

2) I need a yellow cap.

- Aim: Understanding colors and clothes
- Level: 3rd grade
- Material: clothes line, clothes pegs
- Procedure:
    - · Divide the class into two teams.
    - · Two students from each team come to the front and hold the ends of their clothes line.
    - · The first student of each team comes to the teacher. The teacher says to them what he/she needs.
    - · Each student goes back to their team. Find the things and hang them on the clothes line with pegs.
    - · The student who hangs all the things on the clothes line first wins a point.
    - · The second student of each team comes to the teacher and continues the game.

3) Where are they?

- Aim: Understanding prepositions
- Level: 3rd/4th grade
- Material: Grid for prepositions
- Procedure:
    - · Give out the following grids to students. Pictures are drawn in the grid instead of words.
    - · The teacher repeats the positions of objects like these: 'On the desk. . . On the desk. Under the bed. . . Under the bed. . . ')
    - · And then, the teacher says the positions of the objects.

· Students write the sentence numbers in the correct squares.

· After students finish writing the numbers, the teacher checks the students' work. When the teacher says the number, students say the sentence using the grid.

- Example: *Number 1: A ball is on the bed. On the bed.*
  Number 2: A puppy is behind the chair.

	Box(in)	Bed(on)	Table(by)	Chair(behind)	Desk(under)
Cap					
Ball					
Book					
Puppy					

(based on Halliwell, 1995, p. 44)

4) What's your favorite subject?

- Aim: Understanding '. . .likes (doesn't like). . .'
- Level: 3rd/4th grade
- Material: Table for survey
- Procedure:
  · Give out the following table for a survey to students.
  · The teacher says whether a student likes a subject or not. Then, students mark the correct blanks with '○' or '×.' depending whether the student likes a subject or not.
  · After listening, the teacher checks students' results like this:
    T: S1, tell me which subjects Chulsu likes and doesn't like.
    S1: Chulsu likes English, science and music, but he doesn't like history and math.
    T: Very good.
    Everybody, do you understand?
    S: Yes.

Name	English	History	Science	Maths	Music
철수	O	X	O	X	O
수미					
인호					

5) Jerry is in the living room.

- Aim: Understanding 'Someone is in the . . .'
- Level: 3rd/4th grade
- Material: Picture cards
- Procedure:
  · Stick a picture of a house on the board, and then put a living room, bathroom, bedroom and kitchen on the board beside it.
  · Then, introduce Daddy, Mommy, Sunam, Sujin, and Jerry.
  · Now, the teacher tells where Daddy is, then students put Daddy in the right room.
- Example:
  T: Where is Daddy? He's watching TV. Can you guess? Where is he? He's in the living room.

6) How's the weather?

- Aim: Understanding 'How's the weather?' and 'It's cloudy. . .'
- Level: 3rd/4th grade
- Material: Picture cards for the weather
- Procedure:
  · Give out picture cards to students.
  · The teacher says the weather.
  · Then, students put up the right picture card and do a motion previously taught according to the weather.

- Example:

  T: It's very hot. Get your hat and put it on.

  S: ______________________________________.

7) You are animals.

- Aim: Understanding the sounds of animals
- Level: 3rd/4th grade
- Material: Picture cards of animals
- Procedure:
  - · Work in groups of four or five.
  - · Distribute animal picture cards to each group.
  - · Let us pretend we are animals.
  - · The teacher makes a sound that an animal makes.
  - · Students hold up the right picture card and repeat the right sound that the animal makes.
- Example:

  Bees buzz buzz.

  Mice squeak squeak.

  Frogs ribbit ribbit.

  Birds tweet tweet.

  Hens cluck cluck. (Roosters cock-a-doodle-doo cock-a-doodle-doo)

  Sheep baa baa

  Ducks quack quack.

  Turkeys gobble gobble.

  Dogs woof woof.

  Cats miaow miaow.

  Pigs oink oink.

  Horses neigh neigh.

  Cows moo moo.

  Elephants trumpet trumpet.

  Lions roar roar.

8) Let's pretend we are animals

- Aim: Understanding the movement of animals
- Level: 3rd/4th grade
- Material: Picture cards of animals
- Procedure:
    - · Distribute animal picture cards to each group.
    - · Let us pretend we are animals.
    - · The teacher puts up each card, and says how each animal moves.
    - · Then the teacher moves like an animal.
    - · Students hold up the right picture card and do the right movement that the animal makes.
- Example:

  A horse gallops.
  A worm wriggles on the ground.
  A puppy bounces.
  A monkey swings in the tree.
  A rabbit hops.
  A mouse creeps.
  A sea gull glides.
  A kangaroo jumps.
  A lion stalks.
  An elephant stomps.
  And I walk.

9) What's missing?

- Aim: Memorizing the names of the objects
- Level: 3rd/4th grade
- Material: Picture cards of objects

- Procedure:
  · Stick the pictures on the blackboard.
  · Ask the students to name the objects.
  · Ask the students to close their eyes.
  · And then hide a picture.
  · Now, students open their eyes and look 'What's missing?'
  · The students guess what is missing.

10) 1-2-3-4 Freeze

- Aim: Counting numbers from one to twelve
- Level: 3rd/4th grade
- Material: None
- Procedure:
  · Choose one student to be 'It.' Tell the student to face the wall. And the others stand at 'Start.'
  · The student who is 'It' counts like this:
    1 - 2 - 3 - 4 - 5 - 6 . . . Freeze!
    1 - 2 - 3 - 4 . . . Freeze!
    1 - 2 - 3 - 4 - 5 - 6 - 7 - 8 - 9 - 10 . . . Freeze!
  · Every time he says 'FREEZE', 'It' turns around towards the other students and checks if anyone is moving.
  · The other students can freely walk towards the student ('It'), but they must stop when they hear the word 'FREEZE'.
  · If 'It' sees someone moving, 'It' calls their names and they are 'out' and go back to wait at 'Start.'
  · The first student who touches 'It' on the back wins the game.
  · One of the students who is out is the next 'It,' and they play the game again.
- Example:
  'It': S1, you touched me on the back.
  You win the game.

S: Let's play more.

'It': Who's the next 'It?'

You three do 'rock-paper-scissors' and decide the next 'It.'

(based on Argondizzo, 1992, pp. 88~89)

2. Speaking games

1) Snowball game

- Aim: Practicing 'I want to be. . .'
- Level: 5th/6th grade
- Material: None
- Procedure:
  · Make groups of five to six students.
  · The first student (S1) says what he/she wants to be. . . when he/she grows up.
  · The second student (S2) says what S1 wants to be. . Then, says what he/she (S2) wants to be. .
  · When students forget what others have said, students can say, 'Excuse me, (student's name). What did you say?'
- Example:
  S1: I want to be a doctor.
  S2: Taehan wants to be a doctor. And, I want to be a teacher.
  S3: Taehan (S1) wants to be a doctor. Sunam (S2) wants to be a teacher. And, I (S3)⋯⋯.

2) Survey

- Aim: Asking and responding 'Do you like. . .?'
- Level: 3rd/4th grade
- Material: Table for survey

- Procedure:
  · Each student meets five students around the classroom.
  · Ask your classmate what his/her favorite sports are and fill out the table.
  · Please ask, 'Do you like. . .?' and answer, 'Yes, I do or No, I don't.'
  · After the activity, you can report your results to the class like this: Sumi likes badminton, volleyball, and tennis, but she doesn't like soccer, and basketball.
- Example:

Name	Soccer	Basketball	Volleyball	Tennis	Badminton
Chulsu	O	X	O	X	O
Sumi	X	X	O	O	O
Inho					
Youngmi					

3) How's the weather?

- Aim: Practicing 'It's snowing' and 'Let's make a snowman.'
- Level: 4th/5th
- Material: Dice for weather, dice for the activity
- Procedure:
  · Make two teams of two students.
  · Give out dice for weather and dice for the activity to teams: Weather dice (It's snowing / It's cold / It's sunny / It's raining / It's hot / It's windy), Activity dice (Let's make a snowman / Put a sweater on / Let's ride a bike / Put your boots on / Put a sunhat on / Let's fly a kite)
  · Do rock-paper-scissors and decide their turns.
  · One student (A1) from the first team (A) throws the weather die. And, make a sentence to match the picture of the weather. If what he/she says is right, team A gets one point.

· The other student (A2) throws the activity die. And, make a sentence to match the picture of the activity. If what he/she says is correct, team A gets one point.
· And, if the weather die and the activity die match, Team A get two more points, so four points in total. Team A's turn ends.

4) Weather forecasters

- Aim: Practicing 'It's raining. . .' and 'Get your umbrella.'
- Level: 4th/5th grade
- Material: Picture cards for different kinds of weather (umbrellas, scarves, woollen hats, sun hats, paper fans, boots)
- Procedure:
  · Divide the class into three groups. One group (G1) will be 'children in the playground.' And two groups (G2, G3) pretend to be 'weather forecasters'. One group (G2) has the 'good weather' picture cards, and the other (G3) has 'bad weather' ones.
  · The weather forecaster groups (G2, G3) put up a weather picture card by turns.
  · The children in the playground (G1) shout like this using the objects according to the weather forecasts:
    Raining : 'It's raining, it's raining! Get your umbrella.' (They open their umbrellas.)
    Cloudy : 'It's not raining, it's not raining! Close your umbrella.' (They close their umbrellas.)
    Snowing : 'It's snowing, it's snowing! Put your gloves on.' (They put their gloves on.)
    Sunny : 'It's sunny, it's sunny! Get your sun hat.' (They put the sun hat on.)
    Windy : 'It's windy, it's windy! Put your scarf on.' (They put their scarves on.)
  · Students switch from one group to another. The game should be performed quickly.

(based on Argondizzo, 1992, pp. 74~75)

5) Board game

- Aim: Asking and responding 'What do you do. . .?'
- Level: 4th grade
- Material: Board for jobs, place markers, coins
- Procedure:
  · Make two teams of two students.
  · Do 'rock-paper-scissors' and decide their turns.
  · Throw a coin. Heads, move your marker two squares ahead. And tails one square.
  · One student (A1) of the first team (A) throws a coin. And moves their marker according to heads or tails.
  · The second student (A2) asks, 'What do you do?' A1 answers using the picture in the square. If both the question and the answer are right, they can move their marker. But if they are not right, they can not move. They should move their marker back to the original position at the beginning of their turn.
  · The first team's turn ends.
  · The team who arrives at the finish first wins the game.
- Example (1):

  A1: We're first. Flip the coin.

  A2: Heads! Let's move our marker ahead two squares.

  A1: Good! What does he/she do?

  A2: He's an engineer or He works for the Minji company or He works in a restaurant.

  Team B: You're right. Now, it's our turn.
- Example (2):

  Go ahead 1 square; Go back two squares; Go back 1 square; Whose turn is it?; It's your/my turn; Go ahead; Flip the coin; Move your marker ahead/back one square/two squares; That's right/wrong; We win.

6) Find twins

- Aim: Practicing '. . . going to + place'
- Level: 5th/6th grade
- Material: Picture cards of places
- Procedure:
  · Give students a set of picture cards drawn 4 places among 6 places like the park, the zoo, the museum, the library, the supermarket, and the post office.
  · Students talk to their classmates and find a student who has the exact same cards as they do.
  · The students who have found the most students with the exact same cards win the game.
- Example:

  S1: I'm going to the library. Are you going to the library?
  S2: Yes, I am. I'm going to the supermarket. Are you?
  S1: Yes, I am. I'm going to the post office. Are you?
  S2: Yes, I am. I'm going to the zoo. Are you?
  S1: Sorry. I'm not going to the zoo. Bye.

7) Imagine who . . .?

- Aim: Practicing 'Who? How old? Where? Family? Hobbies? Pets?'
- Level: 5th/6th grade
- Material: Pictures or photos
- Procedure:
  · Show students a big photo of a person. They do not know him/her.
  · The teacher writes 'who? how old? where? family? hobbies? pets?' on the board.
  · The teacher invites students to try to guess who he/she is, how old he/she is, where he/she lives, etc. The teacher can talk like this:

    T: Who is he? What's his name? Just imagine. Bob, Tom, Jack?
    S1: David.

T: David. He looks smart.

How old is he? Nine? Ten?

S1: He's eleven.

T: Where does he come from? Where does he live?

· Then, give students time to guess and fill in the blanks.

· After students finish the table, the teacher encourages students to talk about the photo.

	who?	how old?	where?	family?	hobbies?	pets?
철수	David	10	Canada	2 sisters	skating	a puppy
수미						
민호						

- *T: Who can tell us about the photo?*

  S1, thanks.

S1: (Looking at the table) This is David. He is eleven years old. He lives in Canada. He has two sisters. He likes to skate. He has a cute puppy. His name is Happy.

T: Well done! Everybody, who is he?

S: David.

T: Right. This is David. I wonder what his hobby is.

S: Skating.

T: Good! He enjoys skating. How about you?

8) Find someone who . . .?

- Aim: Socializing with classmates
- Level: 5th/6th grade
- Material: Survey
- Procedure:
  · Give out a survey to each student.
  · Talk to your classmates and find the students who . . .

· The students who have talked to the most classmates and fills out their survey first win the game.
· Please Do: Talk your classmates and find out who. . .
· Please Don't Do: Don't cheat from your classmates' papers. Don't overhear what your classmates' are saying.

- Example:

Find Someone Who ~

1. ______________________________ likes ice cream.
2. ________________________ lives in Dongseohak-dong.
3. ______________________________ has two brothers.
4. ______________________________ plays the guitar well.
5. __________________________ enjoys reading cartoons.

9) Who is this?

- Aim: Describing your friends
- Level: 5th/6th grade
- Material: None
- Procedure:
    · Divide the class into two teams.
    · First, do rock-paper-scissors and decide who goes first.
    · One student on team A describes a student on team A. Team B guesses which student.
    · If team B answers right, team B gets one point. And, team B does the same for team A.
    · If team B answers wrong, team B loses one point. And guesses which student again until team B finds the student.

10) Who am I?

- Aim: Asking and responding 'Are you . . .? / Do you . . .?'
- Level: 5th/6th grade
- Material: Photos of famous people
- Procedure:
  · Divide the class into two teams.
  · The teacher hides a photo. And says, 'Who am I?'
  · Each team guesses the answer by turns using 'Are you. . .?' or 'Do you. . .?'
  · If it's very difficult to guess, teacher can give students a clue.
- Example: (The teacher is Barack Obama, US president.)

T: I'm American. I'm a man.

Team A: Are you a singer?

T: No, I'm not.

Team B: Are you an actor?

T: No, I'm not.

Team A: Do you have blond hair?

T: No, I don't.

Team B: Do you play basketball?

T: Yes, I do..

Team A: Uh. . . .

T: My wife's name is Michelle.

11) Information gap activity

- Aim: Asking and responding 'Where is . . .? / It's next to . . .?'
- Level: 4th/5th grade
- Material: Picture cards
- Procedure:
  · Work with your partner.
  · Each student gets a picture of a room with furniture and a second set of

furniture.

· Each student wants to put each piece of furniture where it is located in his/her partner's room.

· Each student asks his/her partner where the furniture is and puts it in the room.

· After the game's over, they compare their pictures.

- Example: *Where is the chair? -> It's next to the door. / Is the chair next to the door? -> Yes, it is.*

12) What do you think about that?

- Aim: Responding 'Wh - ? '
- Level: 5th/6th grade
- Material: Picture cards of places
- Procedure:

  · Make groups of 3 - 4 students.

  · The teacher presents a topic to students, and each group thinks of possible answers.

  · The group which creates the most possible answers wins the game.

- Example:

  · *What's Su-mi doing at the beach?*

  → *She's swimming.*

  → *She's reading a book.*

  → *She's rollerblading.*

  → *She's surfing. . .*

13) Hot seat

- Aim: Asking and responding about a given topic
- Level: 4th/5th/6th grade
- Material: None
- Procedure:

· Make teams of 4 - 5 students.

· The teacher writes a topic to discuss. Students have already learned about the topic in class.

· The teacher gives each group time to think about the topic.

· Each group predicts questions and possible answers.

· Decide the first team (team A) to sit on the hot seat.

· The leader of team A sits on the hot seat, facing the class. The other members of team A stands around the hot seat. They can help their leader once.

· The other teams ask questions by turns until the leader of team A can not answer.

· Team A gets the points of the number of questions that team A answered correctly.

- Example: (Topic: What did you do last Sunday?)

  B: What did you do in the morning?

  A: I went to the supermarket.

  C: Why. . .?

  A: Because I wanted to buy something.

  D: What did you buy?

  A: Some eggs, potatoes and meat. . .

3. Reading games

1) Making words

- Aim: Making words using the alphabet
- Level: 4th/5th/6th grade
- Material: Letter cards
- Procedure:

  · Make groups of 3 -4 students.

· Put 15 letter cards face down on the table.

· After the teacher says, "Go!," each group arranges the letters to make a word.

· The group which makes the most words within a time limit wins the game.

- Example: book, clock, computer, lamp, map, pen, stapler, telephone, window

2) Hangman

- Aim: Practices of words and 'Are there . . .?'
- Level: 4th/5th grade
- Material: Words
- Procedure:

  · Make groups of 4 students.

  · One student (S1) thinks of a word. And, makes one blank for each letter in the word and draw a gallows beside it.

  · Another student guesses a letter that might be in the word. If he/she guesses correctly, S1 writes the letter(s) in the correct blank(s). The person gets to make one guess as to what the word is. If he/she does not guess a letter correctly, draw one body part of the hanging person. A head, then a body, 2 arms, 2 legs, 2 feet and 2 hands.

  · Each student can guess the letter like this: 'Are there any ' ---(s)?'

  · If the students guesses the word right before the person is hanged, they win the game. Then, S1's turn ends.

3) Word Bingo

- Aim: Reviewing the learned vocabulary
- Level: 4th/5th grade
- Material: Bingo board, word cards, glue sticks
- Procedure:

  · Give out a set of 16 word cards to children.

  · Make groups of 3 - 4 students.

· Each student glues word cards any place on the bingo board.

· The teacher says a word, and each student circles the word.

· If he/she makes 4 circles in a row down, or across, or diagonally, he/she says, "Bingo!"

· The group which has the most Bingoes wins the game.

- Example:

father	man	mother	cap
map	uncle	doctor	girl
son	brother	teacher	student
look	aunt	sister	boy

4) What color are they?

- Aim: Matching the objects to the color cards
- Level: 4th/5th grade
- Material: Color cards, word cards
- Procedure:

· Work in pairs.

· Give out a set of color cards and a set of word cards to each pair of students.

· One student puts a color card and a word card on the desk. Then reads the word. If the word on the card can be the color on the color card, he/she gets one point.

· They take turns.

5) Go fish

- Aim: Reading furniture words
- Level: 5th grade
- Material: Furniture word cards

- Procedure:
  - · Make groups of 3 - 4 students, 48 cards altogether.
  - · Give out 4 sets of 12 furniture word cards.
  - · Each student gets 4 word cards, and puts the others in a pile face down on the desk. S1 chooses one card in their hand and talks to the next student (S2).
  - · You can talk like this:

    S1: (to S2) Do you have a table?

    S2: (If S2 has the card, S2 gives it to S1.)

    (If S2 doesn't have the card) No, I don't. Go fish.

    S1: (Picks up a card from the pile on the table.)

    (If he picks the word table,) I picked a table! (S1 shows the card to the other players and ask another question)

    (If S1 doesn't pick the word table, S1's turn ends. S2 asks a question to S3.)
  - · Any student who has four of the same cards puts them down on the table face up.
  - · The student who has the most furniture word sets wins the game.

6) What have you seen?

- Aim: Familiarizing objects in the classroom
- Level: 5th/6th grade
- Material: Objects (or picture cards) in the classroom
- Procedure:
  - · Choose 10 classroom objects and cover with a towel or cloth.
  - · Uncover for a minute, and ask students to look at them carefully.
  - · After a minute, cover again and ask them to write the names of the objects in three minutes.
  - · The student who has written the most names right wins the game.
- Examples of objects: *pen, pencil, crayon, book, notebook, eraser, glue, ruler, chalk, stapler, wallet, keys, glasses, umbrella, watch, cassette, etc.*

7) What are you wearing?

- Aim: Describing what your classmate is wearing.
- Level: 6th grade
- Material: Picture cards, sentence cards
- Procedure:
  · Make groups of 3~4 students.
  · Give out a set of nine picture cards of clothing words and a set of nine sentence cards to each group.
  · Line up 9 sentence cards in three rows. And, put nine picture cards in a pile on the desk.
  · The first student takes the picture card at the top then chooses a sentence card. If they match, he/she gets the pair. If they do not match, put the sentence card back in place. And put the picture card at the bottom of the picture card pile.
  · The student who has the most pairs wins the game.
- Example: *He is wearing a red T-shirt and jeans. / She is wearing a yellow dress and a red hat. / She is wearing a pink blouse and a green skirt. . .*

8) The memory game

- Aim: Understanding the past forms of verbs
- Level: 6th grade
- Material: Verb word sets (present, past)
- Procedure:
  · Make groups of 3 - 4 students.
  · Give out a set of 12 present tense verb word cards and a set of 12 past tense verb word cards to each group.
  · Each group puts the two sets of word cards in two rows face down on the desk apart from each other.
  · The first student picks one card from each group and says the words. If they have the relationship of present vs. past, he/she makes a sentence using the past

tense form of the verb and keeps them.

· If they are not related, put the cards back in their original places.

· The student who has made the most sentences wins the game.

9) Going down the ladder

- Aim: Reading sentences for future dreams
- Level: 6th grade
- Material: Ladder
- Procedure:
  · Work with your partner.
  · Go down the ladder and make a sentence like the example.
    Ex) Top: Mi-ra - Bottom: doctor
    → Mi-ra wants to be a doctor.

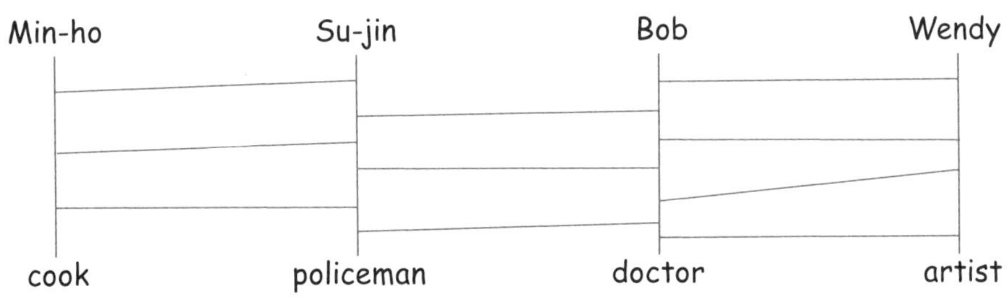

10) Concentration

- Aim: Understanding the past forms of verbs
- Level: 6th grade
- Material: Sentence cards ('Why -?' / 'Because -.')
- Procedure:
  · Make teams of 4 students.
  · Each team makes sentence pairs using the sentence cards of 'Why - ?' and

'Because -.'

· One team calls another team and reads a "Why -?" card. The second team answers with a 'Because -' card. If the answer is not reasonable, the first team wins.

· Each team takes turns.

11) Going down the ladder

- Aim: Building simple sentences
- Level: 6th grade
- Material: Ladder for making sentences
- Procedure:
  · Make groups of 3 - 4 students.
  · Give out a ladder for making sentences to each group.
  · The first student picks a word at the top step and pick another word at the next step etc. Then makes a sentence using the words in the order from top to bottom.
  · The other students make sentences like the first student does.

- Example:

I He They You She
are am is can
have going now bright to happy
buy stones watch to the
buy give play visit some beautiful
delicious soccer his her with
friends hometown balls apples cousins

4. Writing games

1) Relaying the alphabet letters

- Aim: Writing the English alphabet
- Level: 3rd grade
- Material: None
- Procedure:
  · Make groups of 6 students and line up behind each other in front of the board facing away.
  · The first student of each group comes to the teacher. The teacher shows them a letter.
  · Each student writes the letter on the back of the next student.
  · Each group relays the letter to the end.
  · The last student of each group comes to the board and writes the letter on the board.
  · The first correct letter gets a point.
  · The first student goes to the other end of the line. Play again.
- Variation:
  1) Palm writing: Write a letter on the palm of his/her friend.
  2) An alphabet letter writing race (based on Slattery & Willis, 2001, p. 84)

T: OK, put your bag under your chair. Now two teams over here. One team this way. Good. One, two, three, OK. Eh, Sumin, what's your team's name?

Sumin: Pink.

T: OK, the pink team. And Ellen, what's your team's name?

Ellen: Orange.

T: OK, the orange team. Now do you know what we are going to do? You're going to write the *a b c*'s. Now one person at a time. a first and then back to the end of the line and the next one writes *b* and go to the end of the line and you have to do the whole thing until you're finished. The whole. . .*a b c d e f g h*. . .all the way to z. So, use your finger. Ah, now pink and orange. OK, ready. . . Good, up behind the line. Come on. Good. One, two, three go. Now *a* first. .

2) Deciphering the code

- Aim: Matching the capital letters to the small letters
- Level: 4th/5th grade
- Material: A code quiz
- Procedure:
  - · Make teams of 3 - 4 students.
  - · Write the following letter code and the quiz.
  - · Leaders of each team comes to the board.
  - · Figure out the code quiz. And write the answer and do as it says.
- Example: Letter code and code quiz

※	℃	£	¥	♂	♀	∠	⊥	≡	☆	◇	△	∵	℉	→	←	↔	√	∽	∴	♤	♡	♧	≠	÷	¤
A	B	C	D	E	F	G	H	I	J	K	L	M	N	O	P	Q	R	S	T	U	V	W	X	Y	Z

←→≡℉∵   ∴→   £⊥♤△∽♤

________   ____   __________

3) Chain Relay

- Aim: Writing familiar words to children
- Level: 4th/5th grade
- Material: Word cards
- Procedure:
  - · Work in pairs.
  - · Tell the students to write a new word which starts with the last letter of the given word. Then use the last letter of the next word, etc.

    Ex) (house → egg → glass → sky →) (date → egg → girl →)

4) Classifying words

- Aim: Understanding word relationships
- Level: 5th/6th grade
- Material: Word cards
- Procedure:
  · Work individually.
  · Read the words in the example.
  · Write the suitable words in the right blanks under the words.
  · Compare their results with their partners.
- Example:
  Ex): mom, windy, cat, jacket, dog, sunny, dad, blouse, cloudy, son, monkey, jeans

animals	family	clothes	weather

5) Information gap puzzle

- Aim: Understanding body words
- Level: 5th/6th grade
- Material: Information gap puzzle, picture cards
- Procedure:
  · Work with your partner.
  · Each student explains the words in English, if possible. Students with lower abilities can point to the correct body parts.
  · Each one takes turns and fills in the blanks.

- Example:

S1: I'll start first. I walk with it. It starts with 'F.'

S2: How many letters does it have?

S1: Four.

S2: I see. It's 'foot.'

S1: Right.

S2: Now, my turn.

I eat with it. This word starts with 'm.'

(Phillips, 1993, p. 91)

6) Color Word game

- Aim: Identifying colored objects
- Level: 3rd / 4th grade
- Material: Color cards, picture cards
- Procedure:
  · Form groups of four or five.
  · Each group gives words related to the color.
  · Each group takes turns and says the word related to the color.
- Example:
  - yellow: *bananas, butter, ...*
  - red: *rose, apple, ...*
  - white: *snow, rice, ...*
  - black: *hair, night, ...*
  - blue: *jeans, the sky, ...*

7) Rules: 'must' and 'mustn't'

- Aim: Understanding 'must,' and 'mustn't'
- Level: 5th/6th grade
- Material: Cardboard paper, colored pencils
- Procedure:
  · Work in groups of four or five.
  · Invent rules for different places: house, library, park, boat, hospital, museum . . .
  · Help children to brainstorm: What are the rules at home? What do your parents tell you that you must do? What do they tell you that you mustn't do?
- Example:

  LIBRARY RULES
  - *You must talk quietly.*
  - *You mustn't eat or drink.*
  - *You mustn't run.*
  - *You must return books on time.*

8) Writing instructions and notes

- Aim: Writing short notes
- Level: 6th grade
- Material: A4 paper, colored pencils
- Procedure:
  - · Work with the whole class.
  - · Each student writes a short instruction or note and gives it to another.
  - · The child who gets it either follows the instruction or sends a return note to him/her.
- Example:

  Ex 1) Go and hold Jim's hand!

  Ex 2)

Dear Tim,

Draw a picture of a monkey! It's sitting on a box and it's wearing a big hat.

Yours,

Fred

PS: It's a big monkey!

Ex 3)

Dear Mary,

I like your new cap.
Where did you buy it?

Yours,
Sujin

Dear Sujin,

Thank you for your note.
I bought the cap at Happy.
By the way, I like your new blouse.
When did you get it?

Your friend,
Mary

9) Making your own Picture Dictionary

- Aim: Familiarizing new words
- Level: 5th/6th grade
- Material: A4 paper, crayons or colored pencils, magazines
- Procedure:

· Work in pairs.

· First, write the word. Then draw pictures that interests you about the word.

·Finally, write the sentences in English.

· Students with lower language abilities can write the sentences in Korean. Or, they can just write the word.

- Example:

Rabbit
This is a rabbit. Her name is Sally.
She is a very old rabbit.
Sally lives in my garden.

10) Jigsaw story

- Aim: Writing a group story
- Level: 6th grade
- Material: Story book
- Procedure:
    · Make groups of 4-5 students.
    · The first student writes a phrase or a sentence.
    · The second student develops the story by adding a phrase or a sentence.
    · After finishing the story, each group compares their stories with others.
- Example:

A pretty woman with a happy smile
was in the country.
She was riding her horse slowly.

11) Writing puzzles

- Aim: Developing students' problem-solving abilities
- Level: 6th grade
- Material: Picture cards for animals and plants
- Procedure:
  - · Work in groups of four or five.
  - · Each group writes a puzzle collaboratively.
  - · Each group take turns and answers the other groups' puzzles.
- Example:

1) What is it?
   It lives in the sea.
   It has ten arms.
   It does not have any bones.
   It is not a fish!

2) It has eight legs. It is usually black and brown. It makes webs. It eats flies and insects.
3) You can see these animals in the zoo. They love to eat bananas. They live in the trees, jumping from one tree to another. They sometimes act like people.
4) I live in a tree and have two legs. I fly and find food. I like to eat all kinds of worms. I sit on my eggs and sing beautiful songs.

12) Writing poems

- Aim: Writing simple poems
- Level: 5th/6th grade
- Material: A4 paper, colored pencils
- Procedure:

· Work in groups of four.

· Ask students to match the objects in the schoolbags with the word cards.

· Ask each group to write the numbers one to ten (in words) down the left-hand margin of the paper. Check their spelling.

· Encourage each group to make a list of objects in their schoolbags.

· Ask each group to write a poem like 'In my schoolbag,' or 'In my garden,' or 'In my city,' etc.

- Example:

1) *In Tom's schoolbag*
ONE English book,
TWO wooden rulers,
THREE class notebooks,
FOUR black pens,
FIVE chocolate cookies,
SIX paper tissues,
SEVEN white erasers,
EIGHT colored pencils,
NINE bus tickets,
TEN sticky sweets.

(based on Hadfield & Hadfield, 2000, p. 13)

2) Beach holiday checklist
ONE hat,
TWO pairs of shoes,
THREE shirts,
FOUR pairs of trousers,
FIVE pairs of socks,
SIX T-shirts,
SEVEN books,
EIGHT badminton shuttlecocks,

NINE fish hooks,
TEN colored pencils.

(McKay & Guse, 2007, pp. 37~38)

7 Teaching Stories

In this chapter, we will analyze solutions for the following questions about teaching stories in the primary English classroom:

1) Why do we need stories?
2) What are the benefits of stories in the classroom?
3) How can we teach stories in class?
4) What are the characteristics of language in stories?
5) What are the practices of storytelling in primary classrooms?

1. Need for stories

Why do parents and grandparents often tell stories to children? Why do primary school teachers do the same in their classrooms? It is because most of the children are willing to listen to stories. More detailed reasons for stories (Slattery & Willis, 2001, p. 96) are the following:

- Children love stories.
- They are always eager to listen to stories.
- They know how stories work, that is, the conventions of stories through storytelling in the mother tongue.

- They want to understand what is happening.
- They can enjoy listening to stories in English when they start English lessons.
- They enjoy looking at story books by themselves.
- They can reread the stories they like when they can read English themselves.

2. Benefits of stories

What is the real value of stories in the classroom? Based on Brewster (1991) and Slattery & Willis (2001), we will see the value of stories in detail in terms of the four aspects of educational, linguistic, affective, and social values.

1) The educational value of stories

- Stories help children relate new things to what they know already.
- Stories can link English to other subjects across the curriculum.
- The imaginative experiences in the stories can enable children to develop their thinking and creative skills.

2) The linguistic values of stories

Children enjoy listening to stories over and over again. This frequent repetition allows certain language items to be acquired while others are being overtly reinforced.

- Stories can introduce new language in context ideally with pictures and gestures.
- Stories help children become aware of the key words and structures of the language.
- Stories help children acquire intonation and pronunciation by listening.
- Listening to stories develops children's listening and concentrating skills.

3) The affective value of stories

- Stories can help children enjoy learning English.

- Story-telling can let children share their experiences with the group - everyone listens and feels sad or happy.
- Story-telling can help build up children's confidence and encourage social and emotional development.

4) The socio-cultural value of stories

- Stories can introduce children to other cultures.
- Stories can help develop positive attitudes towards the foreign language and language learning, and create a desire to continue learning.

3. How to teach stories in the classroom

How should teachers tell stories to children in their classrooms? Of course there are no right recipes for this. What we can do is pay attention to the L2 researchers' suggestions (based on Brewster, 1991; Morgan & Rinvolucri, 1983; Phillips, 1993) on storytelling.

1) Selection of stories

- Do not choose stories you do not like, or are out of sympathy with.
- Find stories that are relevant to the learning points of the lesson.

2) Time allotment for storytelling

- Decide how long you will spend on the story. Will you use it once or twice or over a period of several lessons?
- Decide when you will read the story. Will you read a little each lesson or all at once after appropriate preparation?
- Decidc what vocabulary to preteach and what you might simply translate during storytelling.

3) Preparation for storytelling before class begins.

- Prepare yourself a skeleton of the story - that is, an outline of the story which contains the language targets of the lesson.
- Practice telling stories out loud using a skeleton before family or colleagues.
- Practice using pictures, puppets, realia, and non-verbal language such as facial expressions, gestures, etc.
- Have children sit around the teacher in a circle, making sure everyone can face the teacher and the illustrations in the story.

4) Storytelling in class

- Do not read the story, just tell it.
- Do not rate the story above the listener: tell the story for the sake of the listener, not for the sake of the story.
- Do not become preoccupied with 'getting the language right' - your telling will become nervous or flat.
- Do not rush it, enjoy it. Tell the story slowly and clearly. Give children time to think, ask questions, look at the pictures, make comments.
- Make comments about the illustrations. When you say a word, point to the illustration at the same time.
- Use gestures, eye contact, facial expressions, and change your voice for different characters as much as possible to keep childrens' attention.

5) Students' pre-, while-, and post-storytelling activities

(1) Pre-storytelling activities

- Ask the children to do the group sharing activities in order for the children to be immersed in a storytelling atmosphere.
- Provide a context for the story and introduce the main characters. Then, elicit key vocabulary and phrases and involve them in predicting and participating in the story as much as possible.
- Provide visual support: use of drawings on the blackboard; cut-out figures; speech bubbles; masks; puppets; realia; flash cards, etc.

(2) While-storytelling activities

- Ask children to make any matching sounds to the particular words.
- Ask the children to mime the story as you tell it.
- Ask children to put the scrambled pictures (or scrambled sentences) in order.
- Ask children to fill in the gapped summary of the story.
- Invite children to repeat the key words by pausing and looking at them with a questioning expression and by putting your hand to your ear to indicate that you are waiting for them to join in.
- Involve your pupils actively by asking students to point to the illustrations, and so on.

(3) Post-storytelling activities

- Ask children to retell the story (Cameron, 2001; Wright, 1997). Retelling the story is very difficult for children. Therefore, teachers can do the following to prompt children:
  (1) Children can put the scrambled pictures in order.
  (2) Children can use the key words or sentence cards as prompts.
  (3) The teacher can mime the story and encourage children to figure out the mime correctly and retell the story.
- Use follow-up activities (Brewster, 1991):
  (1) Find out if there are any rhymes or songs that children can learn to help reinforce the language introduced.
  (2) Children can redraw the characters, create maps showing where the story takes place, think of other possible cover illustrations, and so on.
  (3) Children can be encouraged to create their own masks, hats, and other props, as well as models of streets and buildings, etc.
  (4) Children can create their own 'Picture Dictionary,' based on words from the stories they have read or heard.
  (5) Ask children to engage in role play, dramatization, creative activities, surveys, and so on, using the language in the story.

4. Language use in stories

1) Characteristic language use

Children's stories contain uses of language that are considered typical of poetic texts. Many of these devices (based on Cameron, 2001, pp. 163~166) offer opportunities for foreign language learning.

(1) Parallelism

Parallelism means the repeated pattern of a series of related words, phrases, or sentences. It can create a way into the story for the active children, as well as providing a natural support for language learning by repetition so the children start memorizing or feeling comfortable by hearing a familiar phrase or pattern.

(2) Rich vocabulary

Any simple story can incorporate rich vocabulary 'to describe familiar story book characters,' 'to describe how they moved,' and 'to describe what the heroine did.' Stories also may include unusual words with interesting rhythms or sounds that are onomatopoeic.

(3) Alliteration

Alliteration is the use of words that have the same initial consonants. It can offer a source for developing knowledge of letter sounds.

(4) Contrast

Stories for children often contain strong contrasts between characters or actions or settings. Placing ideas of such clear opposition may well help children's understanding of the story as a whole.

(5) Metaphor

Metaphor is comparison between two objects that do not seem alike or to represent something else.

(6) Narrative / Dialogue

Children's stories consist of two main uses of language, narrative and dialogue. Most stories move between narrative and dialogue. Narrative text concerns the series of events. And dialogue is use of language as it would be spoken by the characters.

2) Examples of language use in stories

We will read the following stories and find examples of language use in stories such as parallelism, rich vocabulary, alliteration, contrast, metaphor, and narrative/dialogue. Not all stories have all types of language use in them. They can be rich by using only a few kinds.

(1) Look out, he's behind you! (Bradman & Chamberlain, 1989)

This is Little Red Riding Hood,
this is her grandmother,
this is the woodcutter,
and this is . . . (the big bad wolf!)

Little Red Riding Hood is going to see her grandmother.
She goes out of the house and down the road.
"Look out, Red Riding Hood! He's behind you!" (Says a rabbit)
"Where?" (Says Little Red Riding Hood.)
(Behind the door) "Yum, she looks tasty!" (Says the big bad wolf)

She goes round the corner. . .
"Look out, he's behind you!" (Says a hedgehog)
"Where?" (Says Little Red Riding Hood.)
(In the trees) "She can't see me! Heh! Heh! Heh!" (Says the big bad wolf.)

Over the bridge. . .
"Look out, he's behind you!" (Says a frog.)
"Where?" (Says Little Red Riding Hood.)
(Behind the flowers) "I can't wait to gobble her up!" (Says the big bad wolf.)

Across the village green. . .
"Look out, he's behind you!" (Says a horse.)
"Where?" (Says Little Red Riding Hood.)
(In the water for horses) "The things I do for a meal!" (Says the big bad wolf.)

And into the dark, dark wood.
"Look out, he's behind you!" (Says an owl.)
"Where?" (Says Little Red Riding Hood.)
(In the wood) "It won't be long now, yummy, yummy. . ." (Says the big bad wolf.)

At last, Little Red Riding Hood goes into grandmother's cottage.
"Look out, he's behind you!" (Says a cat.)
"Where?" (Says Little Red Riding Hood.)
(Behind the door) "At last I'm going to gobble you up. . . Grrr!" (Says the big bad wolf.)

"Help! Save me!" (Says Red Riding Hood.)
Is this the end for Little Red Riding Hood?
"Look out, Mr. Wolf, he's behind you!" (Says a parrot.)
"Where? There's no me there. . . Eeek!" (Says the big bad wolf.)
Who can save her now?
(Behind the door) "Stop, you villain!" (Says a woodcutter.)

Here are Little Red Riding Hood
and her grandmother,
and here is the woodcutter. . .

"Thank you Mr. Woodcutter! (Says grandmother.)
"That's all right, it was nothing." (Says the woodcutter.)
(Under the table) "Isn't there someone missing?" (Says the cat.)

But where is the big bad wolf?
(In the woodcutter's shed.) "Drat!"

▪ Characteristic language use

① Parallelism is found in the first stanza, with the repetition of 'This is . . .' The rest of the paragraphs, except the end, repeats a version of the line 'Look out, he's behind you!' followed by 'Where?' The last stanza repeats the opening stanza's repetition of 'This is . . .' but replaced with 'Here is/are . . .'

② Rich vocabulary is all given to the Big Bad Wolf. He gets to say 'yum' (meaning delicious), 'heh' (indicating a wicked laugh), 'gobble her up' (meaning eating very quickly and sometimes noisily), 'yummy' (another delicious), 'eek' (a noise that means fear and surprise) and 'drat' (a mild bad word).

③ Alliteration is in the names 'Big Bad . . .' (letter B) and 'Red Riding . . .' (letter R).

④ Little Red Riding Hood and the bad wolf are clearly contrasted characters, representing good and evil; the old woman and the young girl contrast youth and age; also helpless (Red Riding Hood) and powerful (wolf and woodcutter). The wolf changes from a position of power to one of helplessness. Perhaps also cunning and artless, as the wolf hides everywhere, the animals see him everywhere but Little Red Riding Hood never sees him until it is too late.

⑤ The forest can be seen as metaphorically representing life outside the safety of the family, and the wolf as representing threats to safety and innocence.

⑥ Narrative/Dialogue are significantly placed. Almost every stanza begins with an action phrase, followed by a dialogue warning line 'Look out!, he's behind you,' rcpeated with 'Where?' Only the conclusion at the end changes slightly as the situation does.

(2) Alva and the Robin (Slattery & Willis, 2001)

Alva is a little girl.
She lives in a house with a lovely garden.
She likes talking and singing and playing with her friends.
But today her friends are away with their families.
She is on her own and feels very sad.
She walks out into the garden - all by herself.
She sees a robin in a tree.
'Hello robin,' says Alva. 'How are you today?'
'Oh, I'm fine. How are you?' says the robin.
'Oh,' says Alva, 'you can speak.'
'Yes,' says the robin, 'and I can sing too.'
'Oh,' says Alva, 'what else can you do?'
'Well, I can fly, of course,' says the robin.
'Oh,' says Alva. 'I can't fly. I wish I could fly. I want to visit my friends.'
'Would you like to meet some of my friends?' says the robin. 'They are here in the garden.'
Alva looks around. 'I don't see anyone.'

'Oh, you have to look carefully.' says the robin. 'Look over there, there's a ladybird.'
'Where?' says Alva.
'Over there,' says the robin, 'under the big green leaf.'
And Alva walks over and picks up the leaf and there's the ladybird.
'Oh, I can see you, ladybird,' says Alva. 'Good morning, ladybird.'
'She's in a hurry,' says the robin.

'And here is a butterfly,' says the robin.
'Where?' says Alva.
'Over there,' says the robin, 'in the flowers.'
And Alva walks over and looks in the flowers.

'Can you see all his colors?' says the robin. 'There's red and yellow and blue and purple and orange and brown.'

'Oh, I can see you, butterfly,' says Alva. 'Good morning, butterfly.'

'And now,' says the robin, 'here are my other friends.'

'Where?' says Alva.

'Over there,' says the robin, 'on top of the tree.'

And Alva walks over and looks in the tree and there are lots of birds.

'Oh, I can see you all,' says Alva. 'Good morning, birds.'

'Now,' says the robin, 'you know all my friends.'

'Thank you, robin,' says Alva. 'I'm having a nice time.'

▪ **Characteristic language use**

① Parallelism in Alva and the Robin are limited and runs in threes. Three times Alva says a version of 'Oh, I can see you . . .' and 'Good morning. . .' to different creatures and repeats the word 'Oh', as does the robin. And the robin says 'Over there. . .' three times too. 'Alva walks over. . .' is also used three times.

② Contrast is shown in the images of a human who has human friends meeting a bird with its friends so different species share a similar situation in that both have friends.

③ Narrative and dialogue exists as Alva and the Robin have a conversation and Alva's actions are described.

(3) The Little Fish Who Wanted to Be Beautiful (Moon, 2000, p.109)

Once upon a time there was a little fish. He lived in a big river with many other fish. But he was not happy. All the other fish were very beautiful. Their bodies were of many different colours, red, blue, green and so on. His body was white. He felt very sad. 'I want to have a beautiful body like those other fish,' he said.

So one day he went to see the king of the river, a big black eel who lived in a big black hole at the bottom of the river. He swam down and down and down to the bottom.

'Who's there?' said a loud voice.
'It's me, little fish,' said the little fish.
'What do you want, little fish?' said the big black eel.
'Please, sir,' said the little fish, 'make me beautiful like the other fish.'
'Hmm, hmm,' said the big black eel. 'All right. What colours do you want?'

'Please make my body red,' said the little fish.
And his body became red.
'Please make my tail yellow,' said the little fish.
And his tail became yellow.
'Please make my fins green,' said the little fish.
And his fins became green.
'Please make my face orange,' said the little fish.
And his face became orange.
'And make my lips red,' said the little fish.
'You rude little fish. You did not say please,' said the big black eel. 'I won't give you any more colours.'

And so the little fish had white lips. But he was very happy because his body had many colours.

He was very beautiful.

▪ **Characteristic language use**

① Parallelism occurs when the little fish makes five requests for the different colors for each part of his body. 'Please make my body red', said the little fish. And his body became red. 'Please make my tail yellow', said the little fish. And his tail became yellow, etc.

② Alliteration is limited to the name of the big black eel, with the repeated sound of the letter 'B'.

③ The contrasts exist between the colorful fish and the plain white fish, as well as the powerful black eel who is the king and the little white fish who asks for a favor, the black vs white and the big and the little descriptions of the two main characters.

④ The narrative is kept mostly to the beginning and the end. The middle has the little fish's requests and the results, 'Please make my body red', said the little fish. And his body became red.

5. Practices of teaching stories in primary classrooms

1) ESL story classes

Example 1: Lion Hunt

(The teacher reads the line and the students repeat it along the actions.)

Going on a lion hunt (echo)
(slap hands on knees then clap hands, alternately in rhythm, throughout poem except where other directions are written)
I'm not afraid (continue slapping and shake head)
Got my hat (grab onto head)
Got my lunch (hold out hand like holding a bag)
Open the door (pretend to open door)
Close the door (pretend to close door)

Going on a lion hunt
I'm not afraid
Coming to some tall grass
Have to get through
Swish, swish, swish, swish (hands and arms part tall grass from middle to side)
Whew, we made it! (wipe brow)

Going on a lion hunt
I'm not afraid
Coming to a roaring river
Have to swim across
Splash, splash, splash, splash (swimming motions)
Whew, we made it!

Going on a lion hunt
I'm not afraid
Coming to a big mountain
Have to hike over
Huh, huh, huh, huh (slap knees slowly, tired voice)
Whew, we made it!

Going on a lion hunt
I'm not afraid
Coming to a large lake
Have to row across
Swoosh, swoosh, swoosh, swoosh (rowing motions)
Whew, we made it!

Going on a lion hunt
I'm not afraid
Coming to a dark cave
Have to creep inside
Tip-toe, tip-toe, tip-toe, tip-toe (whisper as only fingertips touch on knees)
Look to the left (shade eyes and look left)
Look to the right (shade eyes and look right)
Look up (look up)
Look down (look down)
I think I see some BIG eyes (fingers form circles around eyes)

I think it's a...LION! (throw arms back)
Out of the cave...(slap knees)
Across the lake...(row)
Over the mountain...(slap knees quickly)
Across the river...(swim)
Through the grass...(arms part tall grass)
Open the door...(open door)
Close the door...(clap)
Whew, we made it!...(wipe brow, slap knees)

We went on a lion hunt,...(slap knees)
And WE weren't afraid!!!...(shake head)

Questions for discussion

(1) The teacher and children read the story while doing the actions. Do you think the actions are effective for students to understand the story?

(2) What do you think of the story? Is it a good children's story or not?

(3) How important are the sound effects, like swish or splash? How do they contribute to the story?

(4) Do you think the students understand the humor at the end of the story?

Example 2: Retelling The Three Little Pigs (based on Slattery & Willis, 2001, p. 106)

T: OK, what is the first thing that happens in The Three Little Pigs?
S: Once a pig made a house and a fox. . .and the fox. . .blew it. . .
T: Blew it. . .blew it down. OK, that's right. OK, the first pig made his house with? What did he build it with? What did he build that house with?
S: Grass.
T: Yeah. Grass. Straw. He built it out of grass. That's right. And who blew it down?

S: A fox. . .
T: A fox? A wolf.
S: Yes. Yes. A wolf.
T: That's right and the second pig. . .
S: The little pig going to his brother's house.
T: And what did that little pig make his house out of?
S: A wooden house.
T: OK, a house made out of?
S: Wood.
T: That's right. Yes. Wood. Sticks. Branches from the tree. He built his house out of sticks.

Questions for discussion

(1) Have you ever read the story 'The three little pigs'? Do you think it is an interesting children's story? If yes, why?

(2) Retelling the story, how does the teacher help students to remember the story? Do you think they are helpful to the children?

(3) Besides asking questions, what other activities could students do to review the story?

Example 3: Presenting a story-reading lesson (Ong & Murugesan, 2007, pp. 48~49)

T: Story time, everyone.
S: (At story time, the students sit down in the storytelling area.)
T: (The teacher puts a Big Book up on an easel.)
(He reads the title of the story aloud while the children look at the cover.)
(Then, he signals for them to repeat it.)
S: Flipper to the Rescue!
T: What do you think this story is about?
(He asks the students to guess what the story is about.)

S: A fish!

T: Look at that big octopus!

(As he reads to the children, he taps on certain words and pictures in the book with a pointer.)

T: What do you think happens next?

(Sometimes he stops to ask questions and answer them.)

S: He runs away.

S: Flipper chases him.

T: (He covers the words on the last page with a sheet of paper.)

S: (They look at the illustration and try to predict the ending of the story.)

T: Flipper chases the octopus for a long time.

(Then he uncovers the text and finishes reading the story.)

(Afterwards, he encourages his students to talk about the story.)

T: Flipper is brave, isn't he?

S: Yes, he is brave.

Questions for discussion

(1) First, the teacher says, "Story time, everyone." After that, what do students do? Do you think it is a good technique?

(2) How does the teacher present the story? Can you think of any other strategy of presenting the story?

(3) What after reading activities do you think would be useful after this type of presentation?

2) EFL story classes

How do primary English teachers teach stories in their classrooms? We will see an example in the following. Ms. Kim teaches stories based on 'Lesson 4. Wash Your Hands' (MEST, 2009) to third graders.

Storytelling

▶ The title of the book: From Head To Toe

▶ Script

I am a penguin and I turn my head. Can you do it? I can do it!
I am a giraffe and I bend my neck. Can you do it? I can do it!
I am a buffalo and I raise my shoulders. Can you do it? I can do it!
I am a monkey and I wave my arms. Can you do it? I can do it!
I am a seal and I clap my hands. Can you do it? I can do it!
I am a gorilla and I thump my chest. Can you do it? I can do it!
I am a cat and I arch my back. Can you do it? I can do it!
I am a crocodile and I wiggle my hips. Can you do it? I can do it!
I am a camel and I bend my knees. Can you do it? I can do it!
I am a donkey and I kick my legs. Can you do it? I can do it!
I am an elephant and I stomp my foot. Can you do it? I can do it!
I am I and I wiggle my toes. Can you do it? I can do it! I can do it!

(Carle, 2001)

Building Background, Before-activity

T	It's time for storytelling!
Ss	Wow~
T	Can you guess what the story is about?
Ss	Umm..
T	OK. Look at the cover. (showing the book) What do you see? There is a... (point the boy)
Ss	Boy! 아이요!
T	Great! There is a boy. Anything else?
Ss	새요!
T	Good! What is 새 in English?
S1	Bird요! Bird!
T	You got it! A bird! There is a bird. There is a boy and there is a bird.
Ss	Ah..
T	Can you read what the title of this book is?
Ss	Um.. From, head.. to
T	(point the letter 'Toe') From, head, to, ___!
Ss	toe
T	Terrific! (point the title of the book) from, head, to, toe. (slowly) From head to toe! Repeat after me. From
S2	from
T	head
Ss	head
T	to
Ss	to
T	toe
Ss	toe
T	OK. Put them together. From head to toe!
Ss	From head to toe!
T	Can you put your hands on your head?

Ss	(Students do it)
T	Great! Touch your toes, please.
Ss	(Students do it)
T	Wonderful! Let's read this book together!
Ss	Yes!

While-activity

	Pointing to the picture while reading a story
T	Point to the head!
Ss	(follow the teacher's direction)
T	Point to the toes!
Ss	(follow the teacher's direction)
T	Let's read this book now. What's this?
Ss	Penguin! Penguin! It's a penguin....
T	(While reading the book, ask some questions and let students mimic the motions) Ex: The teacher uses the following procedure while mentioning each animal. - Have you ever seen a penguin? - What does a penguin look like? A penguin is a short-legged bird of the South Pole. Penguins have webbed feet and wings. It is a bird but cannot fly. Penguins swim very well. - Do you like penguins? - What is the penguin doing? Shall we do it? (The teacher does the storytelling like the above example.)
T	What's next?

Post-activity

T How was the book? Was it fun?

Ss Yes!

T ▶ Activity 1:

Can you remember what to call this? (pointing teacher's head)

(Practice the names of parts of the body, mimicking the appropriate motions according to the order of the names presented in the story.)

▶ Activity 2:

Practice the names of parts of the body while singing together (Title: Head and shoulders song)

Head and shoulders, knees and toes
knees and toes
Head and shoulders, knees and toes
knees and toes
Eyes and ears and mouth and nose
Head and shoulders, knees and toes
knees and toes

▶ Activity 3: Comprehension questions (Students answer questions, mimicking the appropriate motions)

- Who is in this story?
- Who can turn their head?
- Who can bend their neck?
- Who can raise their shoulders?
- Who can wave their arms?
- Who can clap their hands?
- Who can thump their chest?
- Who can arch their back?
- Who can wiggle their hips?

- Who can bend their knees?
- Who can kick their legs?
- Who can stomp their foot?
- Who can wiggle their toes?
- Who can do all these things?

Questions for discussion

(1) How does the teacher encourage students to guess about the story?

(2) In the while-activity, the teacher asks students to mimic each animal's action. Why do you think the teacher uses this strategy?

(3) The teacher uses the song "Head and shoulders" as one of the post-activities. What other activities can the teacher use?

(4) Would you use a translation of a famous Korean fairy or folk tale? How can this benefit the students?

8 Teaching Role Play

In regards to teaching role play in primary classrooms, we will investigate the following questions:

1) What is the definition of role play?
2) What are the benefits of role play?
3) What are some examples of role play?
4) How do we use role play effectively in the primary classroom?
5) Is there any model procedure for teaching role play in the primary classroom?

1. What is role play?

What is role play? Role play has its place across the school curriculum. What does role play really mean in the language classroom? The following has definitions from some L2 researchers:

- Drama-like classroom activities in which students take the roles of different participants in a situation and act out what might typically happen in that situation (Richards, Platt & Weber, 1985, p. 246)
- In role play the students imagine they are in a specified situation. They may take on the character and role of someone else or be themselves. Pictures can be used to illustrate: the context of the situation (a restaurant); the people involved (a

customer and a waiter); the subject of the communication ('There is no fish but there is beef') (Wright, 1989, pp. 126~127).

- With these techniques: 1) Learners are asked to imagine themselves in a situation which could occur outside the classroom. 2) They are asked to adopt a specific role in this situation. 3) They are asked to behave as if the situation really existed, in accordance with their roles (Littlewood, 1981, p. 49).
- Role plays are exercises where the students are assigned a fictitious role from which he has to improvise some kind of behavior toward the other role characters in the exercises (Paulston & Bruder, 1976, p. 70).
- Role play involves pretending: we ask the students to imagine that they are someone else (a tourist, a customer in a shop) or somewhere else (in the street, at the doctor's). Role play is a way of taking the students out of the classroom for a while and showing them how English can be useful to them in certain situations (Byrne, 1987, p. 39).

In conclusion, as Ladousse (1987, pp. 5~6) puts it, role play has two components, 'role,' and 'play.' In terms of 'role,' when students assume a role, they play a part (either their own or somebody else's) in a specific situation. For example, teacher ↔ student, parents ↔ children, doctor ↔ patient, salesperson ↔ customer, etc. 'Play' means that the role is taken on in a safe environment in which students are as inventive and playful as possible.

2. Why use role play?

Children enjoy role play in the mother tongue. So many teachers try to encourage children to role play. What are the benefits of using role play in the classroom? Let us have a look at the results of many L2 researchers (Harmer, 2001; Ladousse, 1987; Littlewood, 1981; Scott & Ytreberg, 1990; Ur, 1996).

- Role plays can give students the opportunity to practise improvising a range of real-life spoken language in the classroom.
- Role plays do not just use words, but also all the other parts of speaking a

language such as tone of voice, stress, intonation, facial expressions, etc.

- Even beginners can have great fun trying out the little language they know. And, they never worry too much about formal mistakes.
- Role play puts students in situations to build up social skills from a very low level.
- Role play enables children not just to build up social skills, but to practice the language on the basis of classroom interaction.
- Role play helps many shy or hesitant children by providing them with a mask. These children are liberated by role play since they do not have to take the same responsibility for what they are saying.
- It is enjoyable and does not threaten children's personalities, and so increases motivation.
- It promotes interaction in the classroom and children learn to ask as well as respond appropriately.

3. Examples of role play?

As we have seen the definition of 'role play,' in role plays, children might be acting out other persons in real life situations spontaneously. Children can not improvise any given situation in a day. In order for children to be successful in role plays, they need systematic help by beginning with guided role plays to being able to do free role plays (Cross, 1995).

1) Teacher controlled role play

- Children act out the given model dialogue at their desks in small groups.
- Children act out the same language in a new context.
- This type of role play offers rehearsal for later, genuine role plays.

2) Guided role play

First, the teacher exercises direct control over the meanings that are expressed, but not over the language that is used for expressing them. Later, the teacher controls only the situation and the learners' roles in it. Children must create the interaction themselves, on the basis of their roles and the meanings that arise.

Example 1: At the beginning stage, children interact with each other using cued dialogue. Students will normally have their cues printed on separate cards. This gives the interaction some of the uncertainty and spontaneity involved in real communication (Littlewood, 1981, p. 51).

You meet B in the street.	You meet A in the street.
Learner A	Learner B
A: Greet B.	A:
B:	B: Greet A.
A: Ask B where he is going.	A:
B:	B: Say you are going for a walk.
A: Suggest somewhere to go together.	A:
B:	B: Reject A's suggestion. Make a different suggestion.
A: Accept B's suggestion.	A:
B:	B: Express pleasure.

Example 2: Give one child 'cues' and the other 'information.' These are situations where one person needs to gather information or obtain a service, for example: in a travel agency, in a bank, in interviews for jobs, etc.

Student A: You are in a candy store. You can spend 10,000 won. You need to buy candy for your class and your teacher. The teacher wants to eat cotton candy. You must use up as much money as possible.:
Ask what kind of candy there is.

Ask how much each bag of candy is.
Decide what to buy and buy it.

Student B: You are a clerk in a candy store. You have to answer customers' questions and sell candy.
The prices of the candy are:
- jelly beans: 2,000 won
- cotton candy: 1,000 won
- chocolate: 3,000 won
- peppermints: 1,000 won
- gummi worms: 1,500 won

Example 3: Give children a situation and an incomplete dialogue with only questions.

In the Lost Property Office (Byrne, 1987, p. 42)
Student A: You have lost your bag. Go to the Lost and Found to see if anyone has handed it in. Answer the questions the man asks you.

Student B: You are the person who works in the Lost and Found.

A: Er, I've lost my bag.
B: A bag? We've got dozens of bags! What kind of bag?
A: . . . . .
B: What color is it?
A:
B: Is it old or new?
A: . . . . .
B: And what size is it?
A: . . . . .
B: What was in it?
A: . . . . .

B: Oh, and by the way, where did you lose it?
A: . . . . .

Example 4: As learners progress, the teacher controls only the situations and goals. The interaction is in the hands of the children themselves.

Shopping (based on Wright, 1989, pp. 126~127)
Student A: You have a wide selection of pictures of objects which could all be bought in a general store. Each object has its price on it. You are the shop assistant of the store. You must sell the objects to the customers.

Students B, C, D and E: You are customers. Each of you is given a shopping list and twenty thousand won. In turns you ask for one of the items. You must ask for the exact object and its price. You are successful if you can return home having bought everything on your shopping list with the amount of money allowed.

3) Free role plays

- Free role play is role play in the real sense since children have to improvise what they want to say. Each group invents its own stories, and, in the end, each role play is in charge of each child, depending on their collaborative interaction.
- An advantage is that weaker children can restrict themselves to a few simple exchanges, while more able children take advantage of the freedom to be creative and take risks.
- Examples of the guidance
  (1) Orally given context
    - You get lost in the street, and you are looking for your hotel.
    - You are in a library and would like to get a library card.
    - You are going to talk about the tourist attractions of the city at the information desk.

(2) Role instructions

- You want to take a class in soccer / balloon making / basketball. Talk your mother / father into letting you take the class.

4. How to teach role play in the classroom

In most of the classrooms, students are not ready to role play. How can teachers teach role play in the classroom? In the following, based on the role play related references (Cross, 1995; Ladousse, 1987; Wright, 1989) we will try to find effective ways of teaching role play in the primary classroom, focusing on guided role play and free role play.

1) Guided role play

(1) Presentation of a model role play

- A model role play might be performed by a teacher and some volunteer children.
- Or, children might watch a model role play through a CD-ROM.
- The teacher might also write on the board any important phrases or words which the children will need.

(2) Giving out role cards to the children

- Role cards should be concise and contain only the essentials that the children are already familiar with.
- How to distribute the role cards? Teachers can decide who is who or the students can choose, or the distribution can be done at random.

(3) Practicing role play

- Practice role play using the model role play.
- At higher levels, invent role plays using the role cards, and practice the role play.

(4) Performing role play

- Each group performs their role plays at the same time. The only observer is the teacher.
- The teacher observes each group's role plays and notes down the mistakes that he/she would like to review.

(5) Follow-up activities

- Review of the target language: The teacher reviews some critical mistakes that students have made.
- Emotional reflection of the role play.
- Writing their role play in words.
- Inventing new role plays in groups
- Performing role plays if there are volunteers

2) Free role play

(1) Preparation

· Preparation can be done as homework.
· Children choose their partners and their roles.
· Each group invents their story.

(2) Practice of role play

· Each group practices their role plays at home or after lunch, or after class, etc.

(3) Role play before the class

· Each group acts out their role plays before the class using props such as a doctor's gown, his/her stethoscope, etc.
· The teacher monitors each group's performance focusing on both the appropriateness of the interaction and the target expressions.

(4) Make a comparison to the model role play, if possible

(5) Reflection

· Review of the target language.

· Emotional reflection of the role play.

· Writing their role play in words.

5. Practice of teaching role play in the primary classroom

How do primary English teachers teach role play in their classrooms? We will see an example in the following. Ms. Kim teaches 'Role play' of 'Lesson 4. Wash Your Hands' (MEST, 2009, p. 45 (Elementary school English 3)) to third graders.

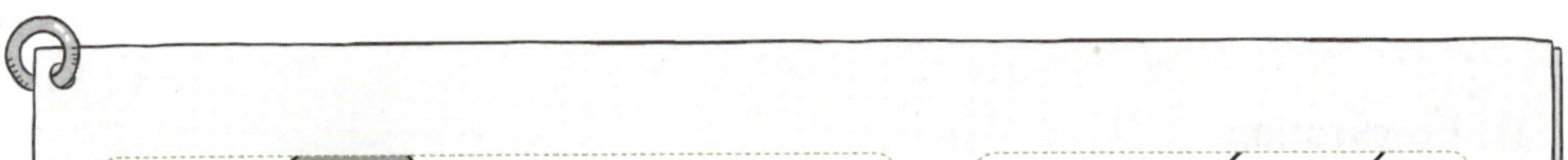

The Beggar & The Prince

(One day, the prince invited the hungry beggar for dinner.)

Prince : (Offering a chair) Sit down, please.
Beggar : Thank you.
(Salivates) I'm hungry.
(Tries to grab food with dirty hands)
Prince : Oh, no. Look at your hands!
Wash your hands.
Beggar : Oh, please. I'm hungry.
Prince : O.K. Open your mouth.
(Puts one piece of pizza in the beggar's mouth.)
Beggar : (Standing up to wash hands after eating pizza) Thank you.
Prince : You're welcome.

Pre-Role play

T	Let's move on to a role play.
Ss	Yeah~!
T	We'll do the role-play by using the expressions you've learnt up to now such as.... (waiting students' reponses)
Ss	Wash your hands! Sit down! Please...
T	Yes, that's right. We have learnt 'wash your hands', 'sit down, please' and so on.
Ss	Open your mouth도 있어요!
T	Great! We have learnt many expressions. Through this role play activity, you'll review what we have learnt in Unit 4.

Ss	OK.
T	First, let's talk about the content related to the picture in the textbook. Open your textbook to page 45. Can you guess what the story is?
Ss	거지와 왕자요! 왕자와 거지요!
T	Good! 'The Prince and the Beggar'. Do you know the story? What's the story about? Take a look at the pictures carefully.
Ss	(Ss tell the story briefly.)
T	What's happening?
Ss	(Ss give their own opinions.)
T	Well done! Let's get started.
Ss	This is group work. First, take a role. Second, make a story. Third, practice it. You can adapt the model script.

While-Role play

T	First, make up a story with your group members.
Ss	(Ss do the activity with their group.)
T	Let's share the story that you made. (T & Ss share the story and T revises some of it.)
T	Excellent! All of you did a great job.
T	(Sorting out the stories and presenting three scripts according to their level)

<Example 1>

Beggar: (knock, knock.)
Prince: Who is it? (Open the door.)
Beggar: I am hungry. Please, give me food.
Prince: Come on in. (Offering a chair) Sit down, please.
Beggar: Thank you.
Cook: This is for you.
Beggar: What's this?
Cook: It's pizza.
Beggar: (Tries to grab food with dirty hands.) Thank you.
Prince: Oh, no! Look at your hands. Your hands are dirty.
Wash your hands first, please.
Beggar: Please, let me eat it. I'm hungry.
Prince: OK. Open your mouth.
(Puts one piece of pizza in the beggar's mouth.)
Beggar: (Standing up to wash hands after eating pizza) Thank you.
Prince: You're welcome. Now, wash your hands, please.

<Example 2> **: Textbook script**

(One day, the prince invited the hungry beggar for dinner.)
Prince: (Offering a chair) Sit down, please.
Beggar: Thank you.
(Salivates) I'm hungry.
(Tries to grab food with dirty hands.)
Prince: Oh, no. Look at your hands!
Wash your hands.
Beggar: Oh, please. I'm hungry.
Prince: O.K. Open your mouth.
(Puts one piece of pizza in the beggar's mouth.)
Beggar: (Standing up to wash hands after eating pizza) Thank you.

	<Example 3>
	(One day, the hungry beggar is invited by the prince for dinner.)
	Beggar: I'm hungry.
	(Tries to grab food with dirty hands.)
	Prince: Wash your hands.
	Beggar: Oh, please. I'm hungry.
	Prince: O.K. Open your mouth.
	(Puts one piece of pizza in the beggar's mouth.)
	Beggar: (Standing up to wash hands after eating pizza) Thank you.
Ss	(Ss practice the role play with their group members.)

Post-Role play

T	Are you done? Now, let's do the role-play in front of the class.
Ss	OK.
T	Here's an evaluation sheet. Take one and pass them on.
	(Hands out the checklist including self-evaluation.)
	Make a checklist during the role play, please.
	Have you all got the checklist?
Ss	Yes.
T	Who goes first?
Ss	Here! Me!
Ss	(One of the groups performs.)
	(Each team performs a role play in front of the class)
T	Terrific! All of you are excellent!
	Now, why don't we watch the screen and compare the story with yours?
	(Show the role play on the CD-ROM.)
T(Q1)	What did the prince say while offering the chair?

Ss	Sit down, please.
T	Good!
	(Keep going)
Q2	What did the prince say when the beggar tried to take the food with his dirty hands?
Q3	How did the prince express that he wanted the beggar to wash his hands?
T	Very good! This time, repeat line by line, please. Let's watch the role play one more time.
Ss	(Repeat line by line)
T	Great! Now, let's role play by switching roles, please.
Ss	(Do the role play)
T	Time's up! Everybody did a great job.
	(Move around the classroom and help Ss.)
	Give the checklist back to me, please.

Questions for discussion

(1) What does the teacher do for the pre-activity?

(2) The teacher sorts out students' stories and present three scripts according to their levels. Do you agree with the teacher? Why or why not?

(3) What does the teacher do for the post-activity? Can you think of any other activity that the teacher can do?

(4) How would you set up a role play for the very first time in class based on introductions?

Part III

Planning Lessons

9. Lesson Plans for Teaching English in Primary Classrooms

9 Lesson Plans for Teaching English in Primary Classrooms

In this chapter, we will examine the following questions regarding good lesson plans for teaching English in primary classrooms:

1) What are the benefits of preparing lesson plans?
2) What are tips for making lesson plans?
3) What are the parts of lesson plans?
4) How can you observe English classes?
5) What does a model lesson look like?

1. Benefits of a lesson plan

Why do teachers write lesson plans for class? What are the advantages for using lesson plans? In the following, we will think of the benefits of lesson plans (based on Cross, 1995; Jensen, 2001).

(1) The lesson plan serves as a map or checklist that guides us in knowing what we want to do next. Teachers will be more relaxed and confident if they follow a clear plan and will not forget anything important.
(2) The plan will enable them to improve their timing for different types of activities and to ensure all materials needed for the lesson are prepared.

(3) A lesson plan with a record of what we did in class serves as a valuable resource when planning assessment measures such as quizzes, midterms, and final exams.

(4) This plan, with your comments and corrections, provides a useful, timesaving reference when you next plan the same lesson.

2. Guidelines for lesson plans

Besides novice teachers, experienced teachers also need good and careful lesson planning. It is not the case that there is only one efficient way of teaching English. To teach English well, we teachers should consider students' abilities, interests and language background, to name a few. That is, there can be many effective ways to teach English to many students from various contexts.

In the following, we will take a close look at some guidelines for effective primary English lessons.

① As a starting point, teachers should present lesson objectives clearly. And give students chances to notice lesson objectives during the class.

② Teachers should give students opportunities to use the target expressions through both mental and physical activities.

③ Classroom activities should be interesting and energetic in order for students not to get bored.

④ Balanced time should be given to each activity. Teachers should not give too much time to a specific activity.

⑤ Using songs or chants can help students be immersed emotionally.

⑥ Teachers should prepare extra activities in case activities end earlier than the expected time.

⑦ Each lesson plan should be changed according to the physical or emotional conditions of the teacher or students and the physical conditions of the classroom.

3. A model of lesson plans

When primary English teachers teach English, they use traditional models of other subject matters. And they also try to teach English through the models of mastery learning, experiential learning, and open education (Pae D-B, 1997, pp. 500~526). In the primary English classrooms, many teachers follow the traditional procedure of 'Introduction - Development - Consolidation' as shown in the following table.

1) Introduction

Introduction, as a lead-in activity, includes checking attendance, small talk on weather or sports, etc, review of the previous lesson, and motivation for today's lesson objectives.

2) Development

Development, as a core activity, consists of the presentation of today's lesson objectives and task activities like pre-task activity, task activity, and post task activity.

3) Consolidation

In the consolidation stage, teachers review today's lesson, reflect on activities, assign homework for the next class, and get students to be prepared for the next class.

Table 1 : Procedure of primary English class (Example)

Step	Procedure	Teacher/ Students Activities	Remarks & Aids	Time
Introduction	· Greeting and roll-call · Review of the previous lesson · Motivation	T: Let's review the names of the colors. Who is wearing a blue sweater? T: Look at people in colored clothes.	· Greet with small talk · CD-ROM	7'
Development	· Stating the aims of the lesson · Presenting the new material · Practice the new material · Games and activities · Song and chant	T: What are we going to learn today? T: (Present the new material using puppets, picture cards, etc.) T: Work with your partners. (Whole - Group - Pair - Individual) T: Let's play a clothesline game.	· Decide the aims with the students · VCR, Puppets, Flash cards, Realia, OHP, Paper hats · Clotheslines, Clothes pegs · CD-ROM	25'
Consolidation	· Summary of this lesson · Reflections on this lesson · Assignment · Goodbye	T: This boy is wearing a blue cap and a red sweater. He is very cute. (Using pictures) T: What do you think about today's lesson? S: Good/Wonderful. T: Can you listen to the tape at home? T: See you later.	· Story book Picture cards · Songs	8'

4. Observation of English classes

When we observe English classes, we can follow the systematic flows of 'preparation activities for classes,' 'class activities,' and 'evaluation activities.' These activities as shown in Table 2 include 'lesson planning,' 'practices of teaching and learning English in the classroom,' 'use of teaching materials,' and 'appropriate evaluation.'

Table 2 : A checklist for observing English classes

Domain	Sub-category	Scale				
		1	2	3	4	5
Lesson Planning (20 points)	1. Validity of lesson objectives					
	2. Selection and organization of the contents					
	3. Appropriateness of activities					
	4. Systematic introduction, development, consolidation and evaluation					
Practice (50 points)	1. Identification of objectives and motivation					
	2. Instruction focused on students' abilities and interests					
	3. Suitable distribution of teacher/students activities					
	4. Degrees of accomplishment of lesson objectives					
	5. Appropriate use of classroom English					
Materials (15 points)	1. Preparation of teaching materials					
	2. Appropriateness of teaching materials					
	3. Use of teaching materials					
Evaluation (15 points)	1. Method of students' error correction in class					
	2. Validity of formative evaluation					
	3. Method of evaluation results					
Total						

(Note. 1: Excellent, 2: Very good, 3: Good, 4: Not so good, 5: Poor)

As you see in Table 2, observers evaluate each domain including its subcategories. And, in terms of 'practice of teaching and learning English in the classroom,' each sub-category is weighted double. Therefore, for example, if an observer scales five in 'identification of objectives and motivation,' the score comes to ten (five X two). In the end, the total score is 100, so lesson planning 20, practice 50, materials 15, and evaluation 15.

5. Examples of lesson plans(6학년 7단원)

Date		Learning skills		Listening, Speaking	Teacher	
Unit	7. My Father Is a Pilot.		Period	1/4	Text	56~57
Subject	To ask and answer about jobs					
Objective	Students are able to listen and speak using expressions about jobs.					
Procedure	① Whole class → ② Group work → ③ Whole class → ④ Group work → ⑤ Individual work					
Material	Teacher	PPT, flash, stamp, ball, stopwatch, worksheet				
	Student	Textbook, Notebook				

Steps	Contents	Teaching-Learning Activities	Time	Remarks & Materials
Introduction	Greeting	• Let's sing a song 'Hello, everyone'. • Greetings * T and Ss can start today's lesson with questions about their daily routines.	3'	° T: teacher ° S: student ° Ss: students * ball ° 전체적으로 인사한 후 공을 던지고 받으며 몇몇 학생들과 개별적인 greeting도 한다.
	Reviewing	• Let's review the last lesson. * Talk about what we want to do now. * Ask and answer what Ss want to do.	2'	
	Motivation	• Let's Guess (Guess who) to motivate with PPT material. ① T shows PPT to motivate Ss. ② Ss have to watch it, think about what the picture is about and connect it with today's lesson.	3'	* PPT * stamp ° 연예인이나 유명인 전체그림의 일부를 조금씩 보여주고 누구인지추측게임을 하며 자연스럽게 학습 주제인 직업과 연결시킨다.(예:유재석의 조각그림, 하는 일)
	Learning point	• Let's see today's learning point. **<Learning point>** Let's listen and repeat the expressions to ask and answer about jobs.	2'	* 공부할 문제
	Learning process	• Let's see the learning process of today's lesson. * Look and Listen * Listen and Repeat (1): Pattern Practice * Let's Play (1) -Say and Act (Speed Quiz) -Ask and Answer (As fast as you can)		* 학습순서안내 * PPT ° 학습목표와 과정을 학생들로부터 이끌어 낸다.

Develop-ment	Pattern Practice	• Look and Listen - Let's listen to the dialog. - Guess what the story is about. * Pre-listening, * While-listening * Post-listening • Listen and Repeat (1) - Pattern Practice: practice the sentences on the blackboard. - T gives key expressions and practices how to say them. - If Ss can speak given sentences, T tries to engage them to make sentences with the target form. Ss have to practice them with T.	5´ 3´	* CD-ROM * Text ◦듣기전,중,후 활동을 통하여 주의를 잃지 않고 학습에 집중할 수 있도록 한다. * Flash * Stamp * 게임설명 ◦ 설명을 잘 듣고 게임을 할 수 있도록 한다. ◦ 게임하는 동안 영어로 묻고 답 할 수 있도록 한다.
	Activity 1	• Say and Act: Speed Quiz - One of the group members tries to explain the given expressions to others. If the rest of them correct the answer, they'll get a point.	10´	*Stopwatch ◦활동 전환시 집중구호 등을 사용하여 주의를 잃지 않도록 한다. ◦정의적여과장치를 낮추기 위해 한국어로 이해를 돕고, 제스추어를 사용하여 설명할 수 있도록 한다.
	Pay attention	• Pay attention - T:"Eyes on me!" (clap twice) - Ss: "Eyes on you!" (clap twice)		
	Activity 2	• Ask and Answer: As fast as you can - S1 asks S2 if his or her mother works and S2 asks S3 the same thing. - Whole class listens to the conversation and repeats after them.	5´	
Consolida-tion	Sum up	• Let's review today's lesson. -Unscrambled words -Review the key expressions.	5´	* Flash * Worksheet ◦ 단원의 첫 차시이므로 발화의 부담을 낮추고 재미있게 표현을 익힐 수 있도록 한다.
	Preview	• Announcing the next lesson and homework - You should learn how to communicate with these expressions. - Prepare a presentation for the next class.	2´	
	Closing	• Saying Good-bye - Sing a song "Good-bye". - Time's up. Bye.		
Evaluation Plan	1. Can students understand the expressions about jobs? 2. Can students use the expressions about jobs? 3. Did they help each other?			

Date		Learning skills	Listening, Speaking Reading	Teacher	
Unit	7. My Father Is a Pilot.	Period	2/4	Text	58~59
Subject	To ask and answer about what they want to be.				
Objective	-Students are able to ask questions and answer about what they want to be. -Students are able to read the expressions about jobs.				
Procedure	① Whole class → ② Pair work → ③ Group work → ④ Whole class				
Material	Teacher	PPT, flash, spinner game board, picture cards, ball, word battleship board, stamp			
	Student	Textbook, Notebook			

Steps	Contents	Teaching-Learning Activities	Time	Remarks & Materials
Introduction	Greeting	• Let's sing a song "Good morning" • Greetings * T and Ss can start today's lesson with questions about their daily routines.	2'	° T: teacher ° S: student ° Ss: students
	Reviewing	• Let's review the last lesson : Spinner Game (Whole class) * Spin the board and answer the questions about the jobs according to it.	3'	* PPT * ball
	Motivation	• Short story ① T shows PPT to motivate Ss. ② T: I will tell you a story about Kungfu Panda. Listen carefully to what the panda wanted to be. -"I want to be a doctor?" song.	3'	* stamp * PPT ° 스피너게임을 이용하여 지난시간 복습과 동시에 학습 동기를 유발하고 자연스럽게 다음활동의 Short story로 안내한다.
	Learning point	• Let's see today's learning point. **<Learning point>** Let's ask and answer what we want to be.	2'	
	Learning process	• Let's see the learning process of today's lesson * Look and Speak * Listen and Repeat -Word Battleship (pair work) * Let's Read - Make a sentence * Let's play (2) - Up and down game		* 공부할 문제 * 학습순서안내

Develop-ment	Pattern Practice	• Look and Speak: Pattern Practice practice the sentences on the blackboard.	2´	* PPT * Flash * Word battleship board
	Activity 1	• Listen and Repeat (2) -Word Battleship (pair work)	7´	◦게임설명 ◦ Let's read와 연계하여 쉽고 재미있는 게임으로 말하기듣기 및 읽기를 통합적으로 사용하도록 유도한다.
		• "Ten little Indian boys" song (Gradually louder, gradually softer)	1´	
		• Let's Read - Make a sentence (Individual or group work) T: Some words will come on the TV screen. You have to arrange them in order and make a sentence. 1, father, a, My, nurse, is 2. police officer, grandfather, a, is, My 3. family, is, my, This 4. a, mother, My, pilot, is	5´	◦ 노래부르며 자리를 정리한다. ◦ 정의적여과장치를 낮추기 위해 한국어로 이해를 돕고, 제스추어를 사용하여 설명할 수 있도록 한다.
	Activity 2	• Let's Play (2) -Up and down (whole class) I want to be a ________.	8´	
Consolida-tion	Sum up	• Let's review today's lesson - What's missing? T: I'll put some picture cards on the blackboard. Then, I'll ask you to close your eyes and I'll hide one of the cards. Finally, open your eyes and figure out which card is missing.	5´	* picture cards. ◦ Pick some students and let them hide a card.
	Preview	• Announcing the next lesson and homework - You are supposed to learn how to communicate with these expressions. -Sing a song related to the next lesson.	2´	
	Closing	• Saying Good-bye -Sing a song "Good-bye". -Time's up. Bye.		
Evaluation Plan	1. Can students ask and answer about what they want to be? 2. Can students read the expressions about jobs? 3. Did they help each other?			

Date		Learning skills	Listening, Speaking, Writing	Teacher	
Unit	7. My Father Is a Pilot.	Period	3/4	Text	60~61
Subject	To ask and answer about what they want to be.				
Objective	-Students are able to ask and answer questions regarding jobs. -Students are able to sing a song regarding jobs. -Students are able to write sentences regarding jobs.				
Procedure	① Whole class → ② Pair work → ③ Whole class → ④ Group work → ⑤ Whole class → ⑥ Individual work				
Material	Teacher	PPT, flash, stamp, mirror, worksheet, video clip			
	Student	Textbook, Notebook			

Steps	Contents	Teaching-Learning Activities	Time	Remarks & Materials
Introduction	Greeting	• Let's sing a song "Good afternoon" • Greetings * T and Ss can start today's lesson with questions about their daily routines.	2'	° T: teacher ° S: student ° Ss: students
	Reviewing	• Let's review the last lesson : "Hot Potato" game * Does your mother work? Yes, she does/ No, she doesn't. * What do you want to be? I want to be a ________.	5'	* PPT * Ball * stamp
	Motivation	• Mime game (whole class or pair work)	3'	
	Learning point	• Let's see today's learning point. **<Learning point>** Let's ask and answer questions regarding jobs	2'	* PPT * Picture cards
	Learning process	• Let's see the learning process of today's lesson * Look and Speak - Mirror Mirror Magic Mirror * Let's sing: "People in my town" - Pop quiz (group work) * Let's write * Let's play (3) - Running Treasure Hunt		°마임게임을 통하여 발화의 부담을 낮추고 재미있게 표현을 익힐 수 있는 분위기를 유도한다. * 공부할 문제 * 학습순서안내

<table>
<tr>
<td>Develop-
ment</td>
<td>Activity 1

Activity 2

Pay
attention

Activity 3</td>
<td>• Look and Speak
: Mirror Mirror Magic Mirror
- T&Ss: Mirror Mirror Magic Mirror!
What do you see?
- T: I see you are studying.
What are you studying?
- T&Ss: Mirror Mirror Magic Mirror!
Does your mother work?
(T shows only S1 the picture card)
- S1: Yes, she does. She is a ________.
• Let's sing a song : Pop Quiz!
- T: It's time for a song! You will sing a song "People in my town". Are you ready?
- (After watching the video clip of the song) T: Pop quiz! How many jobs are there in this song?
- Watch it again and write down all the jobs in the song on the paper. (group work)
- The winner is the team that finds all the jobs in the song.
• Pay attention
- T:"Pay!"
- Ss: "Attention!" (clap twice)
• Let's write
• Let's play (3)
: Running Treasure Hunt (group work)</td>
<td>5′

8′

1′

3′

8′</td>
<td>* 손거울
* 거울 앞에서 자신의 입모양을 관찰함과 동시에 배운 표현을 큰 소리로 친구들 앞에서 말할 수 있게 한다.
*Stamp
* Video clip
* 돌발퀴즈
◦ 노래에 있는 직업을 학생들이 생각나는 대로 자유롭게 말해 보도록 한다.
◦ 다시 한번 기회를 주고 모둠별로 노래에 등장하는 직업의 개수와 직업을 나누어 주는 종이에 적도록 한다. (정의적 여과장치를 낮추기 위해 단어의 철자를 모르면 한국어로 적도록)
*4절지도화지
*worksheet 1
*Worksheet 2
*Sticker</td>
</tr>
<tr>
<td>Consolida-
tion</td>
<td>Sum up

Preview

Closing</td>
<td>• Let's review today's lesson Brain Storming (Individual work or group work)
• Announcing the next lesson and homework
• Saying Good-bye
-Sing a song "Good-bye".
-Time's up. Bye.</td>
<td>3′

2′</td>
<td>* Worksheet 3
◦ 쓰기와 관련된 정리 활동으로 그동안 배운 표현들을 자유롭게 생각해 볼 수 있게 한다.</td>
</tr>
<tr>
<td>Evaluation
Plan</td>
<td colspan="4">1. Can students ask and answer the expressions about jobs?
2. Can students sing a song regarding jobs?
3. Can students write sentences regarding jobs?</td>
</tr>
</table>

<table>
<tr><td>Date</td><td></td><td colspan="2">Learning skills</td><td>Four skills</td><td>Teacher</td><td></td></tr>
<tr><td>Unit</td><td colspan="2">7. My Father Is a Pilot.</td><td>Period</td><td>4/4</td><td>Text</td><td>62~63</td></tr>
<tr><td>Subject</td><td colspan="6">To ask and answer about jobs</td></tr>
<tr><td>Objective</td><td colspan="6">Students are able to ask and answer about someone's job in a real situation.
Students are able to participate in 'Finding Family Game' and 'Bomb Game' joyfully.</td></tr>
<tr><td>Procedure</td><td colspan="6">① Whole class → ② Group work → ③ Individual work →
④ Whole class → ⑤ Individual work</td></tr>
<tr><td rowspan="2">Material</td><td>Teacher</td><td colspan="5">PPT, riddles box, stuff related to jobs, picture cards, team cards, video clip, Willy the dreamer (book), worksheet, stamp, dice, snakes and ladders board</td></tr>
<tr><td>Student</td><td colspan="5">Textbook, Notebook</td></tr>
<tr><td>Steps</td><td>Contents</td><td colspan="2">Teaching-Learning Activities</td><td>Time</td><td colspan="2">Remarks & Materials</td></tr>
<tr><td rowspan="5">Introduction</td><td>Greeting</td><td colspan="2">• Let's sing a song "Hello, everyone"
• Greetings
* T and Ss can start today's lesson with questions about their daily routines.</td><td>3'</td><td colspan="2">° T: teacher
° S: student
° Ss: students
* Stamp</td></tr>
<tr><td>Reviewing</td><td colspan="2">• Let's review the last lesson.
* T: Do you remember what the title is in Unit 7?</td><td>2'</td><td colspan="2">* Picture cards
° 제시하는 카드의 그림에 맞게 직업을 넣어 대답하고 맞으면 반학생 모두 따라한다.</td></tr>
<tr><td>Motivation</td><td colspan="2">* Ss: Does your mother work?
S1: Yes, she does. She is a ______.
• Let's Guess : "Riddles box!"
* T: Here is a riddles box. I'll take out one and you guess what the answer is.
• Let's see today's learning point.</td><td>5'</td><td colspan="2">* Riddles box
* Picture cards
° 마이크, 청진기 등 직업을 유추할수 있는 모형물건이나 그림카드, 폭탄 등을 수수께끼상자에 넣고 활동을 한다.</td></tr>
<tr><td>Learning point</td><td colspan="2"><Learning point>
Let's ask and answer about someone's job in a real situation.</td><td>2'</td><td colspan="2"></td></tr>
<tr><td>Learning process</td><td colspan="2">• Let's see the learning process of today's lesson
* Activity (1): Card game
* Activity (2): Survey game
* Review: Snakes and Ladders
* Story telling: Willy the dreamer</td><td></td><td colspan="2">* 공부할 문제
* 학습순서안내
* PPT</td></tr>
</table>

<table>
<tr><td rowspan="4">Develop-
ment</td><td>Activity
1</td><td>• Activity (1) :Card game (group work)
T: Today, we're going to play a 'Card game' and a 'Survey game'. First, let's play the 'Card game'.
- This is group work. I will give out 6 different job cards to everyone. You can look at only your cards. For example, you have cards in which grandfather is a pilot, mother is a teacher and so on. All you have to do is collect cards in which the job is the same.
- If you have two teacher cards, what kind of job cards do you want to collect?</td><td>5′</td><td>* PPT
* Flash
*Stamp
*게임설명
◦ 자신이 가진 6장의 카드 중 많이 가지고 있는 카드의 직업을 모으는 것이 유리함을 안다.
* 게임 설명 중 질문할 때 한국말 또는 영어로 사용할 수 있게 한다.</td></tr>
<tr><td>Activity
2</td><td>• Activity (2) : Survey game</td><td>5′</td><td>* Worksheet
◦ 조사활동 중 영어로만 사용하도록 독려한다.</td></tr>
<tr><td></td><td>• Review
- Snakes & Ladders Game
- Roll the dice and answer the name of the job.</td><td>5′</td><td>* Snakes & Ladders board
* "Willy the dreamer" book</td></tr>
<tr><td>Story-
telling</td><td>• Storytelling

"Willy the dreamer" by Anthony Browne
T: It's time for storytelling. The title of the book is "Willy the dreamer".
- before-reading
- while-reading
- after-reading</td><td>5′</td><td>◦ 이번단원에서 배운 내용을 종합할 수 있는 책을 선정한다.
◦ 읽기전,중,후 활동을 통하여 영어동화책에 흥미를 가지고 읽을수 있도록 한다.</td></tr>
<tr><td rowspan="3">Consolida-
tion</td><td>Preview</td><td>• Announcing the next lesson and homework - Next time, we will learn Unit 8 "What will you do this summer?".</td><td>2′</td><td>◦노래를 부르며 자리를 정리한다.</td></tr>
<tr><td rowspan="2">Closing</td><td>• Saying Good-bye
- Sing a song "Good-bye".
- Before leaving, all of you ask and answer what you want to be.</td><td>1′</td><td rowspan="2">◦단원의 마지막차시이므로 실제의사소통상황으로 교사가 영어실을 나가는 문앞에서 학생들과 1:1로 한명씩 장래희망이 무엇인지 묻는다.</td></tr>
<tr><td>• Let's review Unit 7.
- Ask students what they want to be.
- Ask what their parents do.</td><td>5′</td></tr>
<tr><td>Evaluation
Plan</td><td colspan="4">1. Can students understand the expressions about jobs?
2. Can students use the expressions about jobs?
3. Did they help each other?</td></tr>
</table>

References

Anderson, A, & Lynch, T. (1988). *Listening*. Oxford: Oxford University Press.

Argondizzo, C. (1992). *Children in action*. New York: Prentice Hall.

Bradman, T. & Chamberlain, M. (1989). *Look out, he's behind you!* London: Little Mommoth.

Brewster, J., Ellis, G., & Girard, D. (1991). *The primary English teacher's guide.* London: Penguin Books.

Brown, H. D. (2000). *Principles of language learning and teaching.* (4th ed.) White Plains: Longman.

Brown, H. D. (2001). *Teaching by principles: An interactive approach to language pedagogy.* (2nd ed.) White Plains: Longman.

Byrne, D. (1986). *Teaching oral English.* London: Longman.

Byrne, D. (1987). *Techniques for classroom interaction.* London: Longman.

Byrne, D. (1988). *Teaching writing skills.* London: Longman.

Cameron, L. (2001). *Teaching languages to young learners.* Cambridge: Cambridge University Press.

Carle, E. (2001). *From head to toe.* Bt Bound.

Cross, D. (1995). *A practical handbook of language teaching.* Hertfordshire: Phoenix ELT.

Ediger, A. (2001). Teaching children literacy skills in a second language. In M. Celce-Murcia (Ed.), *Teaching English as a second or foreign language* (3rd ed.) (pp.153~169). Singapore: Thomson Learning.

Flowerdew, J, & Miller, L. (2005). *Second language listening.* Cambridge: Cambridge Press.

Grabe, W. (1991). Current developments in second language reading research. *TESOL Quarterly, 25*(3), 375-406.

Hadfield, J. & Hadfield, C. (2000). *Simple writing activities.* Oxford: Oxford University Press.

Hall, N. (1987). *The emergence of literacy.* Sevenoaks, Kent: Hodder and Stoughton.

Halliwell, S. (1995). *Teaching English in the primary classroom.* New York: Longman.

Hancock, M. (2003). *English pronunciation in use.* Cambridge: Cambridge University Press.

Harmer, J. (1998). *How to teach English.* Pearson Education Ltd.

Harmer, J. (2001). *The practice of English language teaching.*(3th ed.) Harlow: Longman.

Hedge, (2000). *Teaching and learning in the language classroom.* Oxford: Oxford University Press.

Hudelson, S. (1994). Literacy development of second language children. In F. Genesee (Ed.), *Educating second language children.* Cambridge: Cambridge University Press.

Jensen, L. (2001). Planning lesson. In M. Celce-Murcia (Ed.), *Teaching English as a second or foreignlanguage* (3rd ed.) (pp.403~413). Singapore: Thomson Learning.

Jo, M-W. & Lee, H-S. (2004). *A dictionary of English language teaching.(영어교육사전)* Pearson Education Korea.

Johnson, K. (1982). *Communicative syllabus design and methodology.* Pergamon Institute of English.

Kim, J-H, Kim, Y-S, Sun, K-S, Oh, M, and Park, S-H. (2010). *A course for elementary English teacher education.* Kwangju: Intelligence Community.

Krashen, S. D. & Terrell, T. D. (1983). *The natural approach.* Oxford: Pergamon Press.

Ladousse, G. P. (1987). *Role play.* Oxford: Oxford University Press.

Littlewood, W. (1981). *Communicative language teaching.* Cambridge University Press.

MaKay, P. & Guse, J. (2007). *Five-minute activities for young learners.* Cambridge: Cambridge University Press.

Ministery of Education, Science and Technology. (2009). *Elementary school English 3, 4, 5, 6.*

Moon, J. (2000). *Children learning English.* Oxford: Macmillan Heinemann.

Morgan, J. & Rinvolucri, M. (1983). *Once upon a time.* Cambridge: Cambridge University Press.

Nation, I. S. P. (2009). *Teaching ESL/EFL reading and writing.* New York: Routledge.

Nunan, D. (1999). *Second language teaching and learning.* Boston, MA: Heinle and Heinle.

Ong, M. F. & Murugesan, V. (2007). *Teaching English to young learners.* Seoul: Compass Publishing.

Pae, D-B. (1997). *English language learning and teaching.(영어교육학 총론)* Seoul: Hankook Publishing company.

Paul, P. (2003). *Teaching English to Children in Asia.* Hong Kong: Longman.

Paulston, C. B. & Bruder, M. N. (1976). *Teaching English as a second language: Techniques and procedures.* Cambridge, MA: Winthrop.

Phillips, S. (1993). *Young learners.* Oxford: Oxford University Press.

Richards, Platt, & Weber, (1985). *Longman dictionary of applied linguistics.* Essex: Longman.

Rivers, W. (1981). *Teaching foreign language skills.* Chicago: The University of Chicago Press.

Rost, M. (2002). *Teaching and researching: Listening.* Harlow: Longman.

Scott, W. A., & Ytreberg, L. H. (1990). *Teaching English to children.* London: Longman.

Scrivener, J. (1994). *Learning teaching.* Macmillan Heinemann.

Slattery, M, & Willis, J. (2001). *English for primary teachers.* Oxford: Oxford University Press.

Underwood, M. (1989). *Teaching listening.* Harlow: Longman.

Ur, P. (1996). *A course in language teaching.* Cambridge: Cambridge Press.

Wright, A. (1989). *Pictures for language learning.* Cambridge University Press.

Wright, A., Betteridge, D., & Buckby, M. (1983). *Games for language learning.* Cambridge: Cambridge University Press.

http://bussongs.com/songs)

http://www.kididdles.com/lyrics)

http://www.songsforteaching.com)

http://www.youtube.com/watch?v=JBXaupIJHr8)

김영태

(현) 전주교육대학교 교수
(현) 글로벌영어교육학회 부회장
한국영어교육학회, 팬코리아영어교육학회 부회장 역임
제6차 중·고등학교 영어과 및 외국어계 교육과정협의위원
공주대학교 영어교육과 졸업
한국교원대학교 대학원 졸업(영어교육 석·박사)

주요저서
제6차 교육과정 고등학교 공통영어(공저)
제6차 교육과정 외국어고 고급실무영어(공저)
영어교육 연구방법(공저)
외국어교육 접근방법과 교수법(공역) 등 다수

Teaching the English Language to Primary Students - Tasks for classroom interaction
초등영어교수법 - 교실 상호작용을 위한 과업

1판 1쇄 인쇄 ‖ 2010년 8월 10일
1판 1쇄 발행 ‖ 2010년 8월 20일

지은이 ‖ 김영태
펴낸이 ‖ 홍정표
이 사 ‖ 양정섭
책임편집 ‖ 주재명
디자인 ‖ 김미미
일러스트 ‖ 김병진
기획·마케팅 ‖ 김현아 노경민
경영지원 ‖ 조기호 최정임

펴낸곳 ‖ 글로벌콘텐츠
등 록 ‖ 제25100-2008-24호
공급처 ‖ (주)글로벌콘텐츠출판그룹
주 소 ‖ 서울특별시 강동구 길동 349-6 정일빌딩 401호
전 화 ‖ 02-488-3280
팩 스 ‖ 02-488-3281
블로그 ‖ http://globalcontents.tistory.com
이메일 ‖ edit@gcbook.co.kr

값 13,800원
ISBN 978-89-93908-15-2 93740